Opening Blind Eyes

Alison and Charles Taylor

New Wine Press

New Wine Press
PO Box 17
Chichester
West Sussex PO20 6YB
England

ISBN: 1 874367 46 9

Any royalties from the sale of this book will be donated to *Opening
Blind Eyes*, a registered charitable trust. This charity is committed
to preparing the way for the proclamation and demonstration of
Jesus' Kingdom.

Typeset by CRB Associates, Lenwade, Norwich
Printed in England by Clays Ltd, St Ives plc.

Opening Blind Eyes

Take 50–100 ordinary people in any church, anywhere. This book shows how God can reveal spiritual dynamics working underneath the surface of everyday lives. By way of illustration, Alison and Charles have drawn upon the honest testimonies of their friends.

Special Acknowledgements

Some of the illustrations we have used refer to 'forgiving and releasing'. We would like to recommend Joff Day's book *Settled Accounts. Learning How to Forgive and Release* published by Sovereign World International.

We also wish to acknowledge James Robison for his insight into the nature of 'strongholds'. *Winning the Real War* by James Robison was first published in the USA by Creation House.

Special Thanks

We would like to express our thanks to all those friends who have given of themselves by way of testimonies for use in this book. We have also appreciated their help with typing, computing and proof-reading.

Many thanks to Sally Wills for her artwork and to David Tomkin of Scantec Repro Limited for the cover design.

Finally, to Anna, Nathan, Ben and Bethany: a special 'thank-you' for your patience, encouragement and enthusiasm.

Contents

Foreword

'And if your right eye makes you stumble, tear it out and throw it from you; for it is better for you that one of the parts of your body perish, than for your whole body to be thrown into hell.' (Matthew 6:29)

Radical discipleship demands action, not just consideration. In fact, it is the only kind of discipleship that Jesus spoke of. Jesus declared that the Kingdom of God would make uncompromising claims on the lives of those who chose to follow Him as disciples.

To be radical does not primarily mean to be drastic, 'over the top' or revolutionary, although it may appear that way to others. Biblical radicalism is about dealing with root issues. For some Christians, church membership and 'spiritual' activity have become substitutes for discipleship. Following Jesus has become more of a corporate experience than a personal encounter. Where this has happened, relationship with God has been substituted by religion.

This book seeks to open our eyes to the root issues that affect our ability and inability to be true disciples of Jesus. He was far less concerned with externals than we are, because He knew the heart of the human problem was the problem of the human heart. If those issues of the heart which challenge God's rule in us are not confronted and dealt with, then we will find it hard, if not impossible, to be His disciples.

My own life has totally changed as a result of sitting down one Sunday afternoon with my wife Elaine, and my friends Charles and Alison. They gently confronted me about some 'blind spots' in my life. We chatted and I gave them 'permission' to open my blind eyes. In the many months following, God enabled me to see inner issues that were hindering and restricting me from the purpose of God for my life. I not only 'saw' the issues, but made war on them. It was a time of spiritual battles, emotional healing and renewing of my mind.

As I began to see the issues in me resolved, we taught the principles in this book to the whole church, starting with the elders and their wives! In all of this, Charles and Alison were not immune. The Lord also had them drink of their own medicine! It is because I have seen them faithful in not only confronting issues in me, but also in themselves, that I know there is integrity in what is written in this book. It is not just 'good theory'.

The fruit in peoples' lives, including my own, has been genuine freedom. My prayer is that you will open your heart to what the Holy Spirit has to say to you personally through these pages.

Joff Day
24/10/95

Introduction

It never ceases to amaze us that someone actually coined the phrase 'gentle Jesus meek and mild', because reading through the Gospels, we are continually faced with a person who said some very hard things. In fact, some things that Jesus said seem so radical and extreme that they are, quite honestly, an embarrassment to us. Yet Jesus was unashamedly confrontational and blunt; in today's colloquialism, He certainly 'called a spade a spade', and then said to His listeners, *'He who has ears to hear, let him hear'* (Matthew 11:15).

In the following chapters we would like to look again at some of Jesus' teaching in the context of being free to follow Him, wherever and however that may be.

We take this opportunity to invite you to look afresh at the dynamics operating in your life. Step back for a short while and take stock. Consider, for a moment, some very basic issues that affect you. Think about where you live, your source of income, family loyalty and pride, your natural and spiritual inheritance, your family traditions and value-systems, your family hurts from the past or aspirations for the future. We raise these issues because they affect us in our walk with God. When taking the radical step of discipleship, they have power and relevance. You may not have seen their influence in your life before – **but God is opening blind eyes.**

Chapter 1

What is a Disciple?

Essentially, a disciple is someone who follows their leader. Jesus was in the business of making disciples yet He did not coerce people to follow Him, nor did He pretend that it would be easy. He advised His 'would-be' followers to think seriously and count the cost:

> *'For which one of you, when he wants to build a tower, does not first sit down and calculate the cost, to see if he has enough to complete it?'* (Luke 14:28)

At the beginning of His ministry, Jesus went about preaching and saying, *'Repent, for the Kingdom of Heaven is at hand'* (Matthew 4:17). Now this is not a popular manifesto for a kingdom by any account, yet the whole nature of Jesus' Kingdom is that when it is embraced, things change. 'Repent' literally means to turn from sin – to have a change of heart, resulting in a change of mind and a change of purpose. When this occurs in a person's life, things cannot stay the same.

Chapter 2

Entering the Kingdom

Jesus makes it clear that a complete rebirth is necessary to enter His Kingdom. He said to Nicodemus, a prospective follower, *'That which is born of the flesh is flesh, and that which is born of the Spirit is spirit ... "you must be born again" '* (John 3:6–7).

Nicodemus was a little confused. Must he enter his mother's womb again? Impossible! He could not grasp that it is Jesus who gives us the right to become children of God. We are 'born again' – *'not of blood, nor of the will of the flesh, nor of the will of man, but of God'* (John 1:13).

Some religious people of Jesus' day thought that they could be baptized without taking the radical step of repentance, but John the Baptist warned them that this was certainly not so. Their change of heart, in turning away from their sins, needed to be evident. They could not assume that they would be blessed simply because Abraham was their father (Matthew 3:8–9).

When it comes to the Kingdom, our lineage and family connections do not guarantee us a place. We need to be born of the Spirit for ourselves.

Chapter 3

Family Matters

When we are born again into Jesus' Kingdom, the Bible teaches that we become children of God (John 1:12). We actually become His sons by adoption (Romans 8:15) and He is our Father. Colossians 1:13 teaches that God has *'from the domain of darkness, and transferred us to the Kingdom of His beloved Son'*. We really do become part of God's family. In Paul's letter to the Romans, he writes:

> *'For all those who are being led by the Spirit of God, these are sons of God ... you have received a spirit of adoption as sons by which we cry out "Abba! Father!" The Spirit Himself bears witness with our spirit that we are children of God, and if children, heirs also, heirs of God and fellow heirs with Christ ... '*
>
> (Romans 8:14–17)

In this chapter, we would like to look again at Jesus' teaching concerning the family. What does this actually mean for us in practical terms? With regard to our own families, does this mean that we are now no longer sons and daughters of our natural parents?

In Luke 9:59–62, Jesus spoke to a prospective disciple:

> *' "Follow Me." But he said, "Permit me first to go and bury my father." But He said to him, "Allow the dead*

to bury their own dead; but as for you, go and proclaim everywhere the Kingdom of God." And another also said, "I will follow You, Lord; but first permit me to say goodbye to those at home." But Jesus said to him, "No one, after putting his hand to the plow and looking back, is fit for the Kingdom of God." '

Again, in Luke 14:26, Jesus turned and said to the multitudes who were going along with Him:

' "If anyone comes to Me, and does not hate his own father and mother and wife and children and brothers and sisters, yes, and even his own life, he cannot be My disciple." '

What are we to make of these words? At first sight, they would appear to contain very harsh sentiments – even to the point of being unloving. Jesus was clearly using hyperbole here, a figure of speech where He was deliberately exaggerating the point to get His message across – but this certainly does not 'let us off the hook'.

In considering the cost of discipleship, Jesus' message is that family loyalty and allegiance are extremely important and fundamental issues. Alongside our own selfishness, He actually viewed them as a serious hindrance. When we have been 'born again', our ultimate loyalty and allegiance belong to God. Matthew 4:21–22 describes how James and John were out in their boat mending their fishing nets with their father. Immediately Jesus called them, they left their boat and their father and followed Him. Their decision was radical.

Many people throughout the world are forced to make radical separations from their natural families when they decide to become Christians. For a Muslim or a Jew, there would be many consequences in turning away from their religious upbringing. For example, they may no longer take part in the religious celebrations that are often family-orientated. Others may be alienated or even

16

imprisoned. However, for those of us who have been brought up in Christian or even agnostic families, the consequences of our radical decision to follow Jesus may not be so apparent.

Family control may be the reason we feel constrained and unable to break free from the person we once were, or were expected to become.

Having raised the issue of 'family control', the context of our thinking is that, throughout the Bible, God's heart is towards the natural family – He ordained it! God's plan is that a man should leave his parents and be joined to his wife (Genesis 2:24). The children of this union should be a joy to them because they are His gift (Psalm 127:3). It is God's perfect intention for everyone to have the commitment of two parents who love them unconditionally. Fathers are called to reflect the image of God who is our loving Heavenly Father. These positive and healthy aspects of good family life will enable children to grow up with healthy emotions, open spirits and receptive hearts (Proverbs 22:6).

As parents, the Bible encourages us to teach our children about God as we go about our everyday lives (Deuteronomy 6:7). We are to tell them what He has done for us (Psalm 78:4–6). God is faithful; His covenant and loving-kindness will continue even for *'a thousand generations'* with those who love Him and keep His commandments (Deuteronomy 7:9). However, the Bible also clearly teaches that Christians are not made in the flesh, because *'That which is born of the flesh is flesh and that which is born of the Spirit is spirit'* (John 3:6). Each successive generation must find God's reality first-hand.

The following testimony illustrates that, even if we are born naturally into a Christian family, we need to be reborn spiritually. We are reborn *'not of blood, nor of the will of flesh, nor of the will of man, but of God'* (John 1:13):

'I have always known that God and my family loved me. I knew that I was loved even before I was born

17

and that God was looking after me. Mum and dad had prayed with me since I was a baby and read me Bible stories and told me about Jesus. When I was very young, I remember them sitting, reading the Bible and praying. They told me that I would have to decide myself if I wanted Jesus to be in my life. I knew that He was in charge of my parents but I needed to make my own decision.

I was in bed one night when I was nearly three years old and my mum was praying for me. I stopped her. I really had decided to trust Jesus for myself! As soon as I was old enough to understand, I started to ask my parents if I could get baptized. I knew that Jesus was real to my mum and dad but He was real to me as well.

When I have been worshipping, the Holy Spirit has come and touched me. I have laughed and laughed. Sometimes, I have started to shake and cry out and the Holy Spirit has shown me where I need to say sorry and change and be set free.

As I am growing up and have more freedom, I know I have to make more decisions for myself. What sort of person do I want to be? Do I want to be known as a Christian everywhere I go? I know that although I come from a Christian family, I have to decide these things myself. I have decided that I want to keep putting Jesus in charge.'

It cannot be overstated that the passing on of a religious outlook on life, or an allegiance to a particular denomination, does not secure our place in God's family. As the young man found in this next testimony, it may even result in the holding to the outward form of religion while still rejecting its real power (2 Timothy 3:5):

'I was born prematurely, weighing three pounds seven ounces. It was felt highly unlikely that I would live and so the hospital chaplain was called for and I was baptized. Many people have asked me "When did you first attend church?" The answer is that I can't remember when I have not attended church; I was taken in the carry-cot!

Promotion for my father meant a series of rapid moves. We got quite used to it and at the height of our moving, I remember we left a new home before getting all of our tea-chests unpacked. However, in spite of changing homes and schools, we worshipped at the local Anglican parish church each Sunday – this was an accepted part of family life.

I had a good treble voice. From the age of eight I sang in a robed choir and later, when my voice broke, I swelled the ranks of the tenors. At the age of thirteen I became a bell-ringer and spent many happy hours learning to ring the bells. As I became more proficient, I enjoyed visiting new belfries.

Later, I took 'A' level Religious Knowledge at school and had to read the Bible from cover to cover. I had, of course, heard snippets read out Sunday by Sunday but I had not studied it consecutively – I lapped it up!

It had always been my hope to become a primary school teacher and, to my delight, I was accepted at University. With my love of bell-ringing, I was even more delighted to be accepted as a member of the University society of bell-ringers. Sunday by Sunday I rang at the cathedral. After ringing, I would then stay on for the services, but usually found these dry and tedious.

My main subject at college was theology. This caused me to ask some deep questions such as "Is there a God? Can this God be known? What is a Christian?" I was soon to discover the answer.

Many people find faith in Christ through a trauma or when they hit "rock bottom". This was not true in my experience. Things were going pretty well and my discovery of God came as quite a surprise.

By now, I had begun to attend the University Christian Union. It was, perhaps, a little too evangelical for my liking, but I enjoyed listening to the many capable speakers. I was impressed by their warmth. I felt that they had something that I did not have – a personal experience of God.

One evening, a friend invited me to his church, as he was helping with the service. I am so glad I went that night as the passage of scripture read was to change my heart and life. It was Romans 8:9 that challenged me – *"If anyone does not have the Spirit of Christ, he does not belong to Him."* I nearly dropped off my pew! Here was the answer to my question – what is a Christian? Obviously, a person who has the Spirit of Christ dwelling in them. I didn't find it hard to be honest with myself. Christ was not dwelling in my heart and I was not a true Christian.

Two weeks later, after a Christian Union meeting, some friends asked me round for coffee. Just as I was thinking about leaving, one of them said "Let's read from the Bible and pray." The passage was 1 Corinthians 13 – all about love. Then the devastating blow was delivered, "Perhaps you would like to lead in prayer." I assured them that they should pray on ahead and that I would just like to remain quiet! The truth was that I had been "put on the spot". With my Anglican upbringing, I only knew set prayers – they were not too appropriate for use while sitting informally on the floor of a study bedroom! However, in the middle of the prayer time, I prayed aloud that Christ would come into my life by the power of the Holy Spirit and that He would make me a real Christian. The others continued to pray on. A little later I prayed again, "Lord, I don't feel any different but I take You at Your Word and believe You have come in." I was flooded with such joy and I knew, without any doubt, that Christ had come into my life. I said goodbye to my thrilled friends and set off for my digs – praising the Lord in my heart.

The words "Praise the Lord!" and "Hallelujah!" continued to ring in my ears until the early hours of the morning.'

Even those of us who actually have been 'born of the Spirit' as children, while being brought up by Christian parents, still have issues to consider. It is all too easy for us to bring our natural family values and biases into the Kingdom with us, especially if we have (quite rightly) respected our parents and esteemed them. God's purpose for our lives is that we become like Jesus (Romans 8:29). Our parents may have been good models, but we still need to find the expression of His life in us for ourselves.

In this next testimony, our friend was restricted in her walk with God because she had been measuring her life according to her parents' values:

'Being born again at six years old and growing up in a Christian home has definite advantages. It gave me a good grounding in biblical knowledge and safety from many worldly pitfalls. However, it also brought its own disadvantages. I took so many wonderful truths about God and what He had done for me for granted. I also tried to live as my parents did.

Each day, my parents would have "quiet times" alone with God and prayer times together. I grew up feeling a failure because I didn't know how to pray. Reading my Bible daily was a struggle I never conquered. Until I was twenty years old and baptized in the Holy Spirit, I even doubted that I was really saved! My parents do not accept teaching about baptism in the Spirit and view touches by Him as "experiential".

When I left my parents' church, I began to learn how to worship God with more freedom and saw Him move in power. However, I still struggled in my private life. Often I tried – and failed – to discipline myself to have daily "quiet times". Although I was growing in understanding, I was aware that there was a large gap in my life – I didn't really know God. I knew I was saved and I knew He loved me, but I didn't really **know** Him. I still felt a failure and feared I would be exposed as a hypocrite because I didn't measure up to what my parents had modelled.

I began to hear teaching about "religious spirits" and how they seek to limit our view of God and bind us in legalism. One Sunday before the meeting, I was listening to a ministry tape while conditioning my hair. As I lay in the bath, I listened to the speaker talking about religious spirits and I knew that God was talking to me. I decided that I would not let the day pass without getting some prayer to rid me of them. However, I didn't get as far as the meeting; I didn't even get out of the bath! God delivered me there and then – nothing could be less religious than lying in the lukewarm water wearing nothing but a shower cap! For someone who was taught that even lying in bed to pray was irreverent, it was a brilliant release!

Since then, I have had some wonderful experiences with God. As I lay on the floor laughing uncontrollably at one meeting, I saw a picture of my mother's feet as she sat neatly in a pew. "Which do you want?", the Holy Spirit seemed to be asking. "I choose the floor every time, Father!" At other times, the Holy Spirit has come mightily on me and I have just lain in His arms. As I lie there, I know that I am God's child and that I am no failure to Him. I don't have to pray or do anything to gain His love and approval – I just lie there and enjoy His presence. Experiential? – Yes, and I love it!

Recently, I had a wonderful time as I made the beds. I was singing God's praises at the top of my voice, jumping on and off beds and dancing with quilt covers. His presence was so real. My mother would have made the beds and then had her "quiet time". I realized that I had been measuring my Christian life by the wrong yardstick. I repented of trying to be like my parents; I should have been modelling my life on Christ.

That day, I also realized that God doesn't necessarily want me to just have "quiet times". Noisy ones are fine! Religious times motivated by legalism and fear are out – spending my life in His presence is in!'

How about you? Are you living according to family values or expectations, or is your life an expression of a dynamic and personal relationship with Jesus?
Jesus clearly showed honour and obedience to His natural parents (Luke 2:51) and honoured His mother's position by asking John to take her into his household after His death (John 19:26–27). However, on another occasion, when a messenger came to tell Him that His mother and brothers were outside waiting to speak with Him, He said:

> ' "Who is My mother and who are My brothers? . . . whoever does the will of My Father who is in heaven, he is My brother and sister and mother." '
>
> (Matthew 12:48–50)

This is how we are to relate to other believers in the Kingdom – they are part of our 'family' because they are doing the will of God. We are always called to honour our natural families, but we are now God's adopted sons. Our natural family loyalty and allegiance must not cut across the demands of the Kingdom. This fundamental turnaround will mean different things for different people.

For this young woman, although her father meant well, his plans were hindering her from developing into the person God wanted her to become:

'About twelve years ago, father bought a house with adjoining land. He used the land to build houses for each of his children to buy. While this was in progress, I left my husband after a long and painful two years and met a man who lived in a neighbouring town. My dad offered us a house. My boyfriend refused and at the time I had to go along with him because I was carrying his baby. However, I warned him, "If you ever argue with my dad – I'm on his side." I must admit that, at the time, I thought I'd work on him to move. Every time we visited my parents, it included a tour of the wonderful house just waiting for us to have.

Then we became Christians. I still enjoyed seeing my family, the nights out and being together. I loved my home town and hoped to return. I could see nothing wrong with needing to see or phone my parents every few days. My dad was, after all, quite wise in many ways and I thought we should ask his opinion on everything. But God started to show me, bit by bit, the control I was under.

I have done much forgiving and releasing, had much prayer, deliverance and heartache. God is changing me. I used to have my father's temper, his love of money, alcohol problems and was almost continually ill – just like the rest of my family. Now, Jesus is setting me free and I am gradually discovering who I was meant to be; who God wants me to be. My husband has become the head of our house and our relationship is growing. God is helping us to put things in the right order – now my husband has me on his side, should a disagreement arise.

I love my parents very much, but now it is a healthy relationship and I am not pressurized by them any more.'

Sometimes we may feel emotionally obliged to comply with the wishes of our families, because of their own insecurities or weaknesses. In this respect, we all have responsibilities and it is godly that we should fulfil these to the best of our abilities. However, we should not make unreasonable promises or decisions unless we are sure that they are in God's purposes for us. This is even harder if, as in the following testimony, the family is close and protective of itself:

> 'I grew up in a house that was very protective of family times. The absolutely sacrosanct part of the week was Sunday lunch, a time when all the immediate family was required to be present. No one from outside the family was welcome unless they were very old family friends. In particular, girlfriends were not welcome.
>
> When I qualified, started work and met the girl I wanted to marry, my mother was quite difficult with her. When we first announced our engagement, the first response my mother gave was to my fiancée: "Promise me you won't take him off to Africa." (My wife had felt that she was called to go on the mission field.)'

When it comes to being a disciple, Jesus knew that family loyalty would be a real issue. He said:

> ' "Do not think that I came to bring peace on the earth; I did not come to bring peace, but a sword. For I came to set a man against his father, and a daughter against her mother and a daughter-in-law against her mother-in-law." '   (Matthew 10:34–35)

When only one member of a family becomes a Christian, it can cause real division. There will be a clash of two kingdoms in conflict underlying issues in everyday life. Jesus did not intend us to smooth over the issues, or to live under a constant feeling of guilt and inadequacy.

This next lady's experience illustrates that some people actually need to be set free from the emotional pressure of family control:

'My parents were aged forty-two and thirty-eight when I was born. Mother had never intended to increase the family and an attempt had been made to "get rid" of me. However, this failed and I was accepted because my grandmother said, "This child is coming for a purpose." After I was born, a gypsy came to our door and seeing me in my pram exclaimed, "This child is here for a purpose." My mother duly concluded that the "purpose" was as a comfort and companion for her. I was regularly kept from school to accompany her on outings and was expected to live my life "close" to her, sharing much intimate information. Even after I was married, she actually wanted us to live with her, in the same house.

When I refused all this, emotional pressure was put on me – I was being disloyal. She thought me insensitive and ungrateful, saying I had no idea "what this sort of attitude does to a mother."

When I became a Christian, my mother then rationalized that my "purpose" had to be "godly" and she was very proud of the fact. I became known as the "religious one" of the family. I was given a cross to wear because of this and was held in some fear and reverence. This resulted in an aloofness from various members of the family at large.

Since then, God has set me free from the parental control that I was feeling – even after my mother's death. I had been feeling guilty because I had resisted her wishes, even though they had been ungodly. I destroyed the cross I had been given despite its sentimental value.

Now that I am free from the control of my mother's value system, I can see and repent of sinful associations as God reminds me of them.'

Sometimes, we must stand up for our beliefs. This can cause conflict in families, especially, as in the following extract, when the issues are somewhat emotive:

> 'We had to give both of our children Cornish names to comply with the wishes of my husband's family. On a separate issue, when we left their denomination, we were considered outcasts. They challenged us, saying, "Deep in your heart you know where you belong." '

In this instance, the parents were very hurt and offended because their wishes were not fulfilled. Even within Christian families, we must consciously lay down our family control. **We must allow each other to find God's personal direction, despite our natural inclinations and opinions. This is not always easy to do**.

In this next example, difficult decisions were made with integrity and mutual respect between all family members:

> 'It's a privilege to come from a secure, supportive family. In fact, it's a benefit that shouldn't be forgotten. However, from experience, I know that there are times when the support and love of a family can conflict with the personal directive of God.
>
> Both my wife and I come from secure Christian family backgrounds, and we have been Christians for many years. This has not made us exempt from the trials and challenges of life; God has used these to shape and mould us.
>
> During a very difficult time in our lives, we had the opportunity to visit some close friends for an extended holiday. In the evenings, we spent time reading the scriptures and praying together. We earnestly asked the Lord to guide us and show us His will for the future.
>
> One evening, our friend read Genesis 12:1 (GNB): *"Leave your native land, your relatives, and your*

father's home and go to a country that I am going to show you." These words spoke very powerfully. It was as if the Lord was speaking to **me**.

After returning from holiday, it was difficult to carry this out. We thought that within six months we would be leaving in obedience – but it was not that easy.

The responsibilities of working in the family business were clearly pointed out. What would happen if I were to leave? What would happen to the church in which I played an active part? Surely it could not be God's will?

How could we obey the Lord and honour our parents when these options appeared to be mutually exclusive? The tension between these two seemingly incompatible positions was great.

Some close friends were very supportive – others were not. I felt like Jeremiah, *"...your message is like a fire burning deep within me. I try my best to hold it in, but can no longer keep it back."* (Jeremiah 20:9 GNB).

The Lord very graciously pointed out many scriptures as I read His Word, and these gave comfort and strength. He also brought encouragement when it was needed. I received some godly advice – "Let God take care of the consequences of your obedience to Him."

Eventually, the Lord worked everything out so it was possible to leave with my parent's blessing. This does not mean that it was easy for them, but the relationship was intact. In fact, it has since been strengthened.

Instead of leaving in six months, as I had originally thought, it was closer to two and half years. This was the first stage of leaving. We were away for twelve months, during which time the Lord showed us that He wanted us to work overseas.

After a further time of training and preparation, we left to be missionaries in another country. Only a few hours after we had arrived, we attended a small meeting. The speaker read Genesis 12:1. This was the same verse that the Lord had challenged me with several years before. This time it was not a challenge, but in a very gracious way the Lord seemed to be saying, "This is the land I have called you to."

God had not only given His call, but He had also confirmed it. I'm so glad that we were obedient!'

Even with the best family upbringing, certain things may happen that cause us long-standing hurts or hang-ups. None of us are immune to hurt. Mercifully, when we are born again into God's family, it is His will that we receive healing from the ill-effects of our past. He wants to restore our emotions. Sometimes, it's a mystery why we react in the ways that we do – but God knows, and His heart is to reveal the root of the problem.

In this next testimony, as our friend cried out to God, the Holy Spirit solved the mystery of why, for forty years, she had felt so isolated and alone:

'I was feeling really desperate, isolated and totally on my own. Realizing this was wrong, I cried out to God for His help.

My first step in finding a solution was to ask God to show me any people in my life whom I needed to forgive. While praying with friends, the Holy Spirit caused me to recall sensations and feelings as if I were back in my mother's womb. This sounds weird but it was the area that God wanted us to start praying about. As we prayed, the Holy Spirit gave pictures and words of knowledge about my time in utero. My mother had lost one baby and was desperate that I would be born alive. I was aware of grasping and clinging sensations, as though my mother did not want to let go of me and let me be born, in case I died. It seemed as though I had a fear of birth and a fear of death because of that. I also became aware that my father had not wanted me, due to all the traumas from the previous baby's death.

We asked God to come and remove the fears and rejection and to fill me with His presence. The Holy Spirit then showed us that it was physically difficult for me to be born due to the cord being around my neck. We asked God to come and deal with the negative effects. Then, suddenly, there was a sense of release and relief and I felt as though I had been physically born again!

That day, God healed the hurt surrounding my traumatic birth. Now, after forty years of feeling alone, I no longer have that awful sense of isolation!'

Evidently, God may reveal incidents in our lives as far back as our time in utero and even our birth experience. He is interested in every aspect of our lives because He loves us. Some things that may have happened to us within our natural families affect our present ability to function in health and wholeness, but the good news is that Jesus came to set us free! (Isaiah 61:1; Luke 4:18). God is always motivated by His love for us – He longs to heal our hurts and restore our emotions.

As we are open to the Holy Spirit, He may give personal revelation of our past, present or future. Sometimes, this may take us completely by surprise.

In this next illustration, revelation came by way of a dream. However, God did not give the revelation to the young man in question. In this instance, the Holy Spirit chose to reveal it through someone else:

'I had always felt strangely distant and detached. I knew that people had often found me cold and aloof, yet I had no idea of when these feelings first started.

One Sunday morning, John came over to me. Before he spoke, I found myself clutching the wall to stand up. "I had a dream last night," he ventured.

"There was a baby in a glass incubator; its parents wanted to pick it up and cuddle it, but they couldn't."

John had no idea that I had been a premature baby but when he spoke those words to me, it started to open my emotions. I just cried and cried.

God was beginning to heal the hurts I was even too young to know about.'

As God continues to show us past hurts and disappointments, it is necessary for us to forgive those who have caused us pain. As we embrace the Kingdom, God changes us. Previously, we may have felt resentment and anger towards some members of our families because they failed us or let us down. Now, we can feel love and compassion because we know that we have been shown love and compassion by God. Whatever we may feel 'owed' by our natural families, we can truly forgive those who have hurt us in the past.

It is sometimes difficult to realistically face up to the consequences of hurt. However, this next testimony illustrates that facing up to the past can actually bring freedom rather than self-pity. This lady, having painfully counted the cost, was then able to forgive:

'When I was fourteen years old, I became a Christian and I was really filled with joy and excitement. I had been in a meeting for young people and my experience was real.

To my amazement, my mother was unimpressed when I arrived home. I went into the kitchen to tell her and her response was "Don't you get religious mania!"

The following week, I arrived home to find that I had been given the shed in the garden to live in, as my stepfather had decided I was "in the way".

I was counselled by Christian adults that this treatment was "suffering for the Gospel". I accepted this at the time and for years after. However, a couple of years ago, God showed me that I was "owed" because of what had happened. It was only then that I felt the pain and real suffering the rejection had caused me. I realized that I had been sinned against and needed to forgive both my mother and stepfather for this bad treatment – my mother for allowing it and my stepfather for his part. As I forgave them I also released them from their debt to me.'

God does not want us to bury our hurts and suppress our true feelings; nor does He want us to harbour unforgiveness and bitterness. God's heart is to turn the hearts of the fathers and the children towards each other (Malachi 4:6 and Luke 1:17).

'I had grown up from a little girl with my dad as my hero. I loved him and in my eyes he could do no wrong. Nonetheless, I had grown up in an unhappy home environment. My parents rowed constantly, and as a result, I grew up feeling very insecure. From a young age, I had been woken up by the recurring nightmare in which one of my parents was leaving. The way things were, it was inevitable that my nightmare should become reality. I still remember vividly the day my father left. Despite our pleading and begging, he was determined to leave and live with a woman ten years his junior. He had been having an affair for five years. I could not believe he would leave us for her. I felt betrayed and rejected.

For quite a while, I heard nothing from my dad. By the time he got in touch with me, I had heard so many stories about his many years of adultery, I felt I didn't know him anymore. He had all but destroyed my mum who turned to drink for comfort. I looked at what he had done to her, to us and to our family, and I despised him. The saddest thing was that I didn't just hate him for what he'd done. I hated him for who he was.

At first, dad was pleased to be in touch again but it wasn't long before we became an inconvenience. He had a new woman, a new life. He didn't have time to play "dad" anymore. Sometimes when we'd visit, he'd make the excuse that he was just going out and send us away. Other times he wouldn't even bother to come to the door.

It wasn't long before I decided enough was enough. I buried my hurt and pain. I turned it into anger, hatred and resentment and cut him off from my life and my emotions. We sent Christmas and birthday cards but that was the total sum of our relationship.

I carried my hurt and pain inside for years. Then I discovered God. In God, I found the love, acceptance and security I had been looking for all my life – but I couldn't seem to get as close to God as I wanted. One day, God spoke to me and told me why I couldn't get close to Him. You see, I needed to know God as my Father, and without realizing it, I was projecting the type of father my dad had been onto God. As a result, I found it hard to trust God, hard to believe He had the best for me.

God told me that I needed to forgive my dad and release him from the debt he owed me. It didn't all happen overnight. God highlighted issues one at a time and I had to choose to forgive my dad of my own free will. I had to release him from the debt of the love, security and acceptance that he owed me but hadn't given. It cost me a lot to forgive my dad. Yet, as I did, God started to heal me of all the pain and hurt that had been locked up inside me for years. He took my pain, anger and resentment away, and put in me a new heart of love and compassion for my dad.

I guess you'd say "the proof of the pudding is in the eating" and the proof of what God has actually done in me has been proved recently. You see, my dad is ill now. He has Alzheimer's Disease. Sometimes, it takes something awful to happen to someone before they realize what is important in their lives. My dad now regrets the way he has been in the past. He wants to start afresh, to make up for lost time, to begin a new relationship with his children before it is too late. The sad thing is that for my brother, it is already too late. He doesn't know God. He doesn't know about the power of forgiveness. He just can't find it in his heart to forgive my dad for all he's done because he is still hurting so badly from it. Now my brother is hurting my dad in the same way, by rejecting him.

Me? I thank God for forgiveness and for His healing. I thank God I can tell my dad I love him and forgive him, and see just how much that alone means to someone who is so desperate to make amends. More than that, I thank God for giving me the desire of my heart. I am reconciled to my dad and we both have a second chance at being father and daughter again.'

Chapter 4

Inheritance

Although God's heart is to heal the natural family, it is clear from the Bible that family relationships are not eternal (Matthew 22:30). Again, *'That which is born of the flesh is flesh, and that which is born of the Spirit is spirit'* (John 3:6). Similarly, this earth is not immortal; its destiny has already been decided – both the earth and its works will be burnt up and destroyed (2 Peter 3:10).

What about us? What is our personal destiny? The Bible says that:

> *'As for man, his days are like grass;*
> *As a flower of the field, so he flourishes.*
> *When the wind has passed over it, it is no more;*
> *And its place acknowledges it no longer.'*
>
> (Psalm 103:15–16)

We are here on earth for a time and then we die; our body returns to dust and our spirit returns to God (Ecclesiastes 12:7).

Inevitably, one day we will all face physical death, and this may be understood as the permanent separation of the soul from the body. Our bodies will simply rot away and return to dust (Genesis 3:19). But what of our spirit that has returned to God? The Bible teaches that we shall be given a new body at the resurrection and that this resurrection will be for both the righteous and the wicked (Acts 24:15). Then comes the judgement (John 5:29). Ultimate spiritual death may best be understood as the eternal separation of the spirit from God, in Hell; here, there will be eternal punishment (Matthew 25:46).

Many people fear death and are desperate for longevity. For others, their immortality may be conceived as the natural passing on of their biological genes. These genes carry a blueprint for life into following generations. For example, grandparents may take delight in seeing familiar characteristics, looks and little incidental gestures in their grandchildren. These may even remind them of themselves or maybe their own parents or grandparents. There is security in feeling themselves to be the centre of a continuing family line, knowing that the next generation will live on.

Grandchildren are the *'crown of old men'* (Proverbs 17:6), yet these relationships are natural and according to the flesh, having no binding significance after death. In heaven, there is no male or female, no husband or wife (Matthew 22:30). **The idea of re-establishing our natural family relationships after death and into eternity is more allied to spiritualism or ancestor worship than to biblical teaching**.

In the Bible, our fleshly mortality is contrasted with our spiritual immortality. We have been born again, *'not of seed that is perishable, but imperishable'* (1 Peter 1:23). Because of this, Peter exhorts us: *'conduct yourselves in fear during the time of your stay upon earth; Knowing that you were not redeemed with perishable things like silver or gold from your futile way of life inherited from your forefathers, but with precious blood, as of a lamb unblemished and spotless, the blood of Christ'* (1 Peter 1:17–19).

For those of us already in God's family, our spiritual immortality has already begun. As Christians, how we live our lives now will affect how we live our lives eternally. Jesus warns us, *'Do not work for the food which*

perishes, but for the food which endures to eternal life'
(John 6:27).

The concept of immortality is fundamental to the issues
of inheritance. **Because we have been reborn with imperishable seed and our spiritual immortality has already begun,
we can, in the 'here and now', begin to grasp something of
our eternal inheritance of the Age to Come** (Hebrews
6:4–5; Revelation 21:4). In God's family, we are heirs of
the Father and joint heirs with the Son (Romans 8:16–17).
God's will for us is that we should embrace our spiritual
inheritance and begin to possess what is rightfully ours
(Philippians 3:12).

The Bible reveals many parallels between the lives of the
children of Israel and the life of a Christian. In the book of
Deuteronomy, we see that God's purpose was the same
for them as it is for us. His will for them was that they
should come into their promised inheritance. Like ours,
their inheritance was not a reward for their righteousness
(Deuteronomy 9:5–6), but was given according to God's
promise to Abraham (Deuteronomy 1:8). God acted in
His sovereign power to take the children of Israel from
their slavery in Egypt (Deuteronomy 5:15), in the same
way as He rescued us from the *'domain of darkness'*
(Colossians 1:13). As they ventured into the land He had
promised them, to claim their inheritance, God's power
won miraculous victories for them, driving out the previous inhabitants (Deuteronomy 7:1–5, 22–24). Jesus has
already done this for us – He has given us the victory
through His death on the cross (1 Corinthians 15:57). We
are now free to live in the good of His accomplishment for
us (Hebrews 9:11–15; Romans 6:22).

The children of Israel were given certain instructions
to fulfil and God's blessing was conditional upon their
obedience. They were to rid the promised land of its past
idolatrous and pagan practices, removing their pagan
worship sites (Deuteronomy 7:5, 12:2–3). As they did
this, so the blessings of God were released in their lives.
Deuteronomy chapter 28 describes these blessings as

prosperity, health and freedom from oppression. They were to regard these as God's provision. However, they were warned not to take this for granted, or to become conceited, but to remember that it was God alone who had given them the power to make wealth (Deuteronomy 8:17–18). From it, they were to make provision for the poor (Deuteronomy 15:4–11). They were to act righteously in all things, and were to pursue justice so that they might live and possess the land which God was giving to them (Deuteronomy 16:20). As Christians, we have the same mandate.

Just like the children of Israel, we are also to be radical. We must deal with issues in our lives that prevent us being loyal to God. Paul writes, *'Now these things happened to them as an example, and they were written for our instruction ... Therefore, my beloved, flee from idolatry'* (1 Corinthians 10:11 and 14).

We are to be holy, presenting ourselves as a living sacrifice, acceptable to God. We are not to be conformed to this world. Rather, we are to be transformed by the renewing of our minds. In this way, we establish God's will in our own lives – *'that which is good and acceptable and perfect'* (Romans 12:1–2). We are actively to pursue *'righteousness, godliness, faith, love, perseverance and gentleness'*. We are to *'fight the good fight of faith'*, taking hold of the eternal life to which we have been called (1 Timothy 6:11–12). Furthermore, those of us who are rich are warned not to be conceited or to put our hope in material possessions. We are to see our wealth as a provision from God for us to enjoy (1 Timothy 6:17), enabling us to remember the poor (Galatians 2:10) and to serve the needy (Matthew 25:34–46).

Finally, the children of Israel were to be diligent not to allow any former pagan influences to creep back into the promised land. Nor were they to chase after any new gods commended to them by their neighbours (Deuteronomy 6:13–14). If they did not obey this condition, God's blessing was to be removed from them and the curses of oppression and sickness, previously experienced in Egypt, would return (Deuteronomy 8:19–20, 28:58–61).

As Christians, seeking to possess our inheritance in Christ and to live in the good of it, we must be diligent too! We must be careful not to be taken *'captive through philosophy and empty deception, according to the tradition of men, according to the elementary principles of the world, rather than according to Christ'* (Colossians 2:8). God has made us into a *'people for His own possession'* (Deuteronomy 4:20; Titus 2:14). Our inheritance is imperishable and undefiled, and is reserved in heaven (1 Peter 1:4).

But what of our natural family inheritance? In terms of God's Kingdom, and His inheritance for us, is this relevant? Each of us was born into a natural family and are, in one sense, a product of our upbringing. However, when we were 'born again' into God's family, He made us into new creations (2 Corinthians 5:17). This does not automatically nullify our past. Even after our spiritual rebirth, we still inhabit our mortal bodies and often live with the consequences of our former lives. God gives us the gift of His forgiveness (Colossians 2:13–14; 1 John 1:9), but we cannot deny what has gone before.

Whatever our background or heritage, God's heart is to set us free from anything that would prevent us from fulfilling our destiny of being like Jesus (Romans 8:29). God has called us to work out our salvation with *'fear and trembling'* because it is He who is at work in us (Philippians 2:12–13).

In each of our families, characteristics and traits may be passed down from one generation to another – naturally, physically or spiritually. We may have inherited our mother's brown eyes or our father's big feet. A particular family frailty, strength or even a medical condition may have been passed down through our genes. We may also find ourselves portraying some characteristics that are similar to other members of our family. In this respect, it is well known that alcoholism and sexual abuse tend to run in families, the 'abused' later growing up to become the 'abusers'.

We all learn from our parents and are influenced to some extent by their beliefs and value systems. It may come as quite a surprise to realize that some of these may have been founded upon pagan traditions. As Christians, God is calling us to holiness (1 Peter 1:15–16). If our lives have been previously founded upon ungodly principles, we are to repent because God has redeemed us – He has saved us from the *'futile way of life'* inherited from our forefathers (1 Peter 1:18).

Our natural family inheritance may be physical or spiritual. However, if this conflicts with God's plans for us, it will be detrimental to us fulfilling His purposes. In this context, we would be foolish to assume that we can compartmentalize the physical and spiritual sides of life. Physical inheritance, for some, may carry spiritual implications or influence, whereas a spiritual legacy may manifest itself physically. The physical and the spiritual aspects of our being are intrinsically and inextricably linked. We would be wise to consider our natural inheritance in the light of this; **things may not always be as they first appear**.

2 Kings 6:8–17 tells the story of how Elisha's enemies were circling the city and of how his servant was, understandably, afraid. Elisha was not afraid, however, because his eyes were open to the unseen world. The prophet prayed that God would also open the eyes of his servant to see the horses and chariots of fire all around him, protecting him from adversity. The Bible tells us that the Lord opened the servant's eyes and he saw. **Pray that your eyes may be opened to the unseen world operating in your life**, either by direct revelation from God or by the gifts of knowledge, wisdom and prophecy.

We cannot over-emphasize the importance of hearing the voice of the Holy Spirit and this is something that we are all able to do. John chapter 10 tells us that the sheep hear the voice of the shepherd and follow him because they know his voice, but a stranger's voice they will not follow (v. 3–5). Whether we discern the Holy Spirit speaking to us in dreams, visions, pictures, a 'still small voice' or even as an audible voice, He will never contradict the Bible or the principles laid down within it. This must always be our final authority.

By way of illustration, we would like to consider a few aspects of natural family inheritance that will be familiar to most of us in our everyday circumstances. They are neither right nor wrong in themselves; the real issue is whether our natural inheritance is in line with God's will for our lives.

Considering the general lack of employment opportunities, inheriting the family firm is one aspect of natural inheritance that may be welcomed today more than ever before. This can be a real provision from God because it may enable the recipient to earn a living without the initial striving that is sometimes frustrating, costly and time-wasting. However, in the Kingdom, nothing can be taken for granted, because our lives are now under new management. Jesus may have looked like inheriting 'Joseph & Sons – Family Carpenters', but at the age of thirty, full of the Holy Spirit and led by God, He began His life's work!

There are many good things about working in the family business, but we would like to consider those situations that are not so helpful. For example, when we become Christians, our loyalties change. Although our lives should now be founded upon godly principles and righteous living, we may find it difficult to break free from our old way of life.

Some of us may have been brought up in families where honesty has not been strictly practised; for instance, the tax bill may have been cleverly 'adjusted' in some way. This will now have different implications for us, because God has called us to be holy (1 Peter 1:15). We now have to act responsibly, and stand up for what we believe, repenting of our past deceitfulness and dishonesty. **If our**

natural inheritance causes us to continue in sin, it is well worth giving up for the sake of the Kingdom of God.

Inheriting a family business run with integrity may also call for compromise. It may lock us into a situation where we feel 'trapped' or unable to break free from the person we once were, or were expected to become. We may feel obliged to stay in a particular locality or to carry on the family honour or tradition, although our heart is not in it. These aspirations may even be reflected in the names we choose for our children. For example, it may be hoped that John Smith Junior will reflect something of his father in the years to come. If, besides this, he is duly expected to inherit the family firm and to 'step into the old man's shoes', then natural inheritance is simply running its course. This is not wrong, but if God now calls for a radical change of allegiance, lifestyle or location, John Smith Junior may find that he has to reassess the priorities and direction of his life. **A disciple is someone who follows their leader, however and wherever that may be**.

Passing on a family business to the younger generation can also be a heavy burden resting on the parents. As this testimony illustrates, it places expectations and sacrifices on all concerned:

> 'My father had, and still has, an unhealthy desire to keep the family business alive. There are other reasons outside the obvious financial ones – the main one that has had a direct influence over me is pride.
>
> My father's father had a business that he had built up over many years. He was well known in the local council and respected by all who met him. As he grew older, my grandfather looked to my father to take over the business which he duly did. "Stepping into the old man's shoes" I recall hearing when I was younger. I can well imagine my father had the path all laid out in front of him – gain the same respect, move in the same circles – know the same people. He was in the wake of a popular man. The only thing

that they had in common was their name. I recall people calling him "young Roberts" and this was also true of me later. This was not altogether a healthy thing, but making it worse, there became a family pride in being a Roberts. It was not so evident to begin with, but as the business developed and time moved on, it became more prevalent. My father tried to live up to my grandfather's expectations. It was important for him to maintain the family position and, at all costs, to avoid any sort of slur.

It is impossible for me to count the cost for my father but I can talk of the cost to me. For the first eighteen years of my life, I had been fed the traditions of pride, the family name, and even the striving for acceptance by my father. The name was mine to have and to cherish! I can remember being told rather forcibly, "Don't you dare let down the Roberts' name," and at another time, "What would people think if they saw you now?"

Without trying to be blunt, I felt sacrificed to my father's business. Whatever day it was and, seemingly, whatever time it was, my father was never there. I was ill-prepared for living in the world outside education; the only thing I had was several bits of paper, the name of Roberts and a double-dose of pride. It felt as if the foundations upon which my life had been built amounted to nothing. Then God broke in.

After twenty-two years of living with pride, it has not all gone in one quick step. But I have experienced a measure of God's healing, and where there were no foundations, I now have some. Where there was nothing but bitterness, He has given me His love.'

In some families, the parents' own abandoned hopes and aspirations are lived out through their children or their grand-children in the expectation that a long-awaited dream will one day come true. Obviously, these family dynamics are not helpful or advisable. They have absolutely no place in the Kingdom of God, however laudable they may seem. Even in the most well-meaning family, it is possible to feel the victim of somebody else's ambitions. This may appear to have an outworking in the natural, although there may be spiritual implications:

'My godmother is my aunt and I am godmother to her twin boys (I was fourteen when they were christened). We share many physical similarities. My aunt was a nursing sister and cherished the ambition that I would be a nurse too. She took me round her nursing school and introduced me to her nursing tutor when I was fifteen.

At age sixteen, my careers teacher suggested I might like to think of becoming a doctor as she felt I was better suited. My aunt told me I was "aiming high above my station" and would never make it. In my mind, these words seemed to become a curse to me. Even after I had qualified as a doctor, I had a succession of jobs in which I was extremely unhappy. I could never seem to get it right no matter how hard I tried.

I came to the point when I wanted to renounce the ungodly influence over my life that I felt my godmother had been given at my christening. I forgave her for seeking to change my destiny and for exercising that spiritual authority. I also repented of allowing my aunt to try and force me into her mould and to live out her expectations. I told God that I only wanted His plan, and prayed for my mind to be renewed (Romans 12:1–2).

Then some folks gathered for prayer and broke the curse of failure. I actually heard a "snap" when this was prayed over me, following forgiveness of my aunt!'

Be free to discover the will of God for **your** life. Pursue the vision that He has put within **your** heart. This may cause some considerable disruption, in terms of your natural inheritance, or it may cause no disruption at all. **You must make your personal decisions with integrity, because God judges the thoughts and intentions of our hearts**.

Many churches throughout the world are led by families. The older generation are the leaders or pastors and the children, particularly the sons, are 'trained up' to carry on the work. They are both natural and spiritual inheritors. We would be foolish to jump to any hasty conclusions because this may be God's sovereign plan for a particular church. God gives His gifts individually as He chooses (1 Corinthians 12:11). In all likelihood, the leaders will have brought their children up to love and serve God well, sharing the same calling and vision. Nevertheless, where these situations do occur, we would be wise to face up to the possibilities of family pride, selfish ambition and family control. In the Kingdom, fulfilling natural expectations should not be taken for granted!

Many of us inherit a name that has previously been in the family, and as alluded to earlier, these may sometimes be used to denote more than a mere label. Names may signal the continuance of the family line or they may simply be likeable names! Similarly, we may name our children after likeable people, those whom we have loved or wish to remember. Interestingly, when it came to whether John the Baptist should inherit his father's name, God intervened:

> *'The time came for Elizabeth to have her baby, and she gave birth to a son. Her neighbours and relatives heard how wonderfully good the Lord had been to her, and they all rejoiced with her. When the baby was a week old, they came to circumcise him, and they were going to name him Zachariah, after his father. But his mother said, "No. His name is to be John."'*

(Luke 1:57–60 GNB)

Through a vision in the temple, God had clearly told Zachariah what they should call their son (Luke 1:10–13). He was not to be another Zachariah, although his father was a good man – walking blamelessly in all the commandments and requirements of the Lord (Luke 1:6). He was to be called John, having a unique task to fulfil.

Names are sometimes inspired and chosen by God to accord with His purposes (e.g. Hosea 1:1–10). When God inspires a name, it will be a reflection of His perfect will. Whatever the origins of your name, be free to discover the will of God for your life. Pursue the vision He has put within your heart. Consider Saul's change of name to Paul, following his conversion (Acts 13:9).

Names may allude to links with a particular religious belief. For this woman, there was a link between the natural and spiritual that, however intangible, was none-theless real:

> 'My parents were Catholics, and so I was christened into the Catholic church; my name is Mary.
>
> One day, I was sitting at home with the ironing piled up and the beds to change. There was an awesome, pregnant silence that filled the room. I felt compelled to sit and wait. Hours went by. I kept thinking about the name "Mary". I felt uncomfortable and restless. Mary had said "Yes" to God. I loved the name. Mary was a mother figure, someone to intercede; someone to approach for mercy.
>
> The following evening I shared with some friends what I felt the Holy Spirit was bringing. God's presence filled the room. I remember the feeling of heaviness and awesomeness. I was very quiet. I laid down my religious identity with the name "Mary" and all that it had implied to me. Inside, my resolve was changed around. There was a godly sorrow leading to repentance.'

God's heart is to set us free from all aspects of our

inheritance that would hold us in bondage, be it physical or spiritual.

When we eventually die, our body will return to dust and our spirit to God (Ecclesiastes 12:7). People do not leave anything of their spirit here on earth. However, where this does seemingly occur, other spiritual dynamics are at work, from which the inheritor will need release. This was certainly the case for the lady giving this testimony:

> 'Years ago, I had a very strange experience. It was a Saturday morning and I was just waking up in bed. There was a battle going on. My body felt like lead and I could not lift myself up. My head would not move and I felt myself receding into the pillow. I just couldn't wake up. I felt panic. Eventually I became able to move, and noticed that it was just after eight o'clock. Staggering out of my room, I shared my experience with my flat-mates. It was really weird!
>
> Later that morning I phoned my parents. An old aunt who had always lived with us had died earlier that morning, just after eight. I had gone to see her a week previously in an old people's home. As we had said goodbye, her last words to me were "You are my life."'

When we die, our spirit does not live on to outwork in the life of another person here on earth; it returns to God. It is not the human spirit that inhabits other people or places.

Although this concept is an attractive ethereal theme influencing much of art and literature, our sense of guidance and inner strength should not flow directly from the spirit of another. If we feel compelled to follow after someone else's plans, purposes or aspirations, giving our lives over to their influence, then the true nature of this spiritual awakening is questionable.

If we are really following after Jesus, then the Holy

Spirit will be our guide through life; He is the One who discloses to us the plans and purposes of God! (John 16:13)

Similarly, it is not our destiny to live under the influence of anybody else's sin. This is because our destiny is to become like Jesus (Ephesians 4:13). However, the Bible does teach that we are affected by the lives of our families. Exodus 34:6–7 reads:

> *'The Lord, the Lord God, compassionate and gracious, slow to anger, and abounding in loving kindness and truth; who keeps loving kindness for thousands, who forgives iniquity, transgression and sin; yet He will by no means leave the guilty unpunished, visiting the iniquity of fathers on the children and on the grandchildren to the third and fourth generations.'*

This may have been true in Old Testament times but, as 'new creatures' (2 Corinthians 5:17), do the sins of our fathers really affect us? We invite you to consider the following testimony:

> 'I believed I was brought up by my parents to know right from wrong – not to steal, to be honest and to tell the truth no matter what happened. However, the discipline was not consistent, because my father was away from home a great deal with his work. During these years, my mother brought us up. We were a family without a father's constant input. Consequently, I don't recall him sharing anything about how to relate to women or girls.
>
> The earliest recollection I had of sexual feelings and interest in the opposite sex came about by looking at pictures of topless girls from the *Sun* newspaper. I was probably eleven years of age. I remember being rather embarrassed about this, and tried to be as secretive as I could be, keeping the pictures stored in a drawer.

As I got older – into Secondary School – I became more aware that there were other pictures of girls in pornographic magazines. Then I found out that my father kept his own pornographic material. This was conveniently stored in cases above his wardrobe.

As I grew into adolescence, I would see different films on television. My father had his own video player and so we joined a video club. One day I brought home an adult movie – I would have been about seventeen or eighteen years old. My father and I watched this together and I remember his comments of how the film was not that explicit. This was because it was not a "hard core" pornographic film, unlike others my father owned.

During these late teenage years I had little involvement with girls or girlfriends. I did not mix or talk to them, which would have been quite normal. "Normal", to me, was what my father had handed down. This was eventually so well ingrained in my way of thinking, that I had great difficulty in relating to girls in any way other than sexually.

I started dating at nineteen or twenty years of age, but after my first long-term girlfriend, I went from girl to girl, not really respecting the person. I dated younger girls, finding their innocence a sexual attraction.

This selfish gratification of mine continued for years and progressively got worse. What had started with girls in newspapers, then pornographic magazines and pornographic films – then soft porn to hard porn, then dating schoolgirls, finally ended in the worst possible way. I took advantage of a lady who already had great problems in her life. I compounded these problems by indecently assaulting her. My "conscience" had been seared. The persistent sexual self-abuse had made me unfeeling about myself and others.

I did not realize that not only was I deceiving my family and my friends, I was being seriously deceived myself. The nature of deception is that you don't know you are being deceived.

Thankfully, because of the depth of love and kindness from people who have prayed for me, I have seen the issues that had plagued my life, causing such misery, shame and guilt. Many issues have been dealt with forever. The love of God has been shown to me through the honesty, directness and patience of Christian friends. They have been so loving and faithful to me, despite what I had done. I never thought I could be free from such a mess.

I know I am not totally healed or completely sorted. I still fall down in similar areas, sometimes tempted by the enemy at my weakest point. But I am free of the need to watch pornography and am finally laying down the old patterns of using people.

God has and is cleansing me from the past and I know that He is faithful to complete what He has already begun. I have a hope and a purpose in His Kingdom and I am so grateful for His mercy towards me.'

Jesus came to set us free from the effects of the sins of the fathers in our lives. It is important to acknowledge that He did not come to abolish the Law and the Prophets, but to fulfil them (Matthew 5:17). None of us are justified according to the Law, but Jesus has redeemed us from its curse and we are justified through faith in Him (Galatians 2:16).

If we feel that we are not actually free from the effect of someone else's sin, or that we are somehow carrying their load, then we need not feel victimized or disadvantaged. Jesus has set us free (Galatians 5:1). We are to live in the good of what he has accomplished.

Our friend seemingly inherited a guilty conscience...

'I always seemed to be looking over my shoulder. If I was driving at 30 mph in a 30 mph speed limit, I would be checking the mirror to see if there was a police car following! This was not tied to the guilt of having been caught speeding in the past! For that, I had repented before God, received his forgiveness, paid the fine, and driven carefully ever since! But somehow, guilt seemed a part of my life. As much as I asked God to show me if there was anywhere I was guilty, nothing came to mind.

Part of the guilt syndrome was tied to things of a sexual nature. I had made a choice early in my Christian life to stay pure sexually, not getting "involved" with members of the opposite sex until I knew I was ready to marry. When that time eventually came, a short engagement meant that we were able to handle the sexual temptations well, and keep ourselves pure until our wedding night. However, inside, I had a fear of being "taken advantage of" by other women. Because of both the fear and my desire to maintain fidelity within our marriage, I did not relate well to women.

I was amazed, therefore, that at various times in our marriage, I would wake up in the night with an extreme sense of panic and guilt. I thought that the woman in my bed was someone I did not know whom I had sinned with sexually! This paranoia lasted only for a few seconds. When I realized I was married, the woman in my bed was my wife and that, in fact, I had not committed adultery, I was able to sleep in peace!

I spent time praying with some friends and my wife about this issue. My father was illegitimate but this was never discussed openly in the family. It was, in one sense, the family's "guilty secret". I could see that there was a sexually "unclean" streak in my family that I seemed to have fought against person-ally almost all of my life. In our time of prayer, God showed us that "illegitimacy" had affected my life but not at a physical level. It had worked out in other areas of my life, particularly in spiritual things.

During the prayer time, I repented for my grandmother and grandfather's immorality and other sexual immorality in the family, of which I may not have been aware. I also repented of my self-righteous attitude and pride that I had not "fallen" sexually. As the others started to pray and break the power of guilt, God showed me clearly that there are no illegitimate children. The relationship that created such a child was illegitimate, not the child itself. God knew every child that was born even before they were conceived! The sense of guilt that I had done things "spiritually" in an illegitimate way was broken over me. As the ministry time continued, the power of the Holy Spirit overwhelmed the power of guilt and I felt a great load leave.

The very next day, I felt totally different. I felt clean and free. Since then, I have not woken up once with guilty feelings. I have been able to relate to women far better than I ever did before. Jesus said that He had come to set the captives free. He has certainly set me free. Hallelujah!'

Have you considered your inheritance – natural, physical and spiritual?

Open your eyes. Things may not always be what they seem!

Chapter 5

Superstitions and Religious Traditions

An influence may be defined as 'an action invisibly exercised, a dominant, controlling or moral power' (Oxford Dictionary). In this chapter, it is our heart to begin to make more visible the widespread influences of superstitions and religious traditions in the world around us. This will help us see more clearly their effect in our lives.

What is your personal understanding of superstitions and religious traditions? A superstition may be thought of as a practice or opinion based on widely held, but wrong ideas involving the power of the supernatural. A superstition may also involve a belief in magic or a belief that inanimate objects in some way affect our human destiny. A tradition, on the other hand, may be defined as an 'opinion, belief or custom handed down from one generation to another' (Oxford Dictionary). The traditions that we follow will actually affect our social attitudes, beliefs, and ultimately, our behaviour. **In a very real way, traditions bring the influence of past generations into the present time**.

The teachings of the Bible are founded upon traditions that were passed down from generation to generation containing divine revelation from God to mankind.

Someone once came to Jesus asking what they must do to obtain eternal life. His reply was that they must keep the commandments which God had given to Moses

(Matthew 19:16–19). Paul also reminded Timothy that the 'sacred writings' of the Old Testament were able to give him wisdom leading to salvation through faith in Jesus (2 Timothy 3:15). He continued, *'All scripture is inspired by God and profitable for teaching, for reproof, for correction, for training in righteousness; that the man of God may be adequate, equipped for every good work'* (2 Timothy 3:16–17). Paul instructed the disciples in Thessalonica to stand firm and to hold fast to the traditions passed down from the apostles, *'whether by word of mouth or by letter'* (2 Thessalonians 2:15). They were also commanded to be aloof from those who were not following these traditions but were living unruly lives (2 Thessalonians 3:6).

The Bible is, in fact, full of traditions. One main theme is the sharp contrast between the traditions of God and the traditions of men. Jesus brought this contrast to bear when His disciples were criticized for eating with impure hands and for not following the traditions of the elders. He rebuked the Pharisees, saying that although they held to the traditions of men, they actually neglected the commandments of God (Mark 7:8). They were invalidating God's word for the sake of their own tradition. Paul also makes this sharp distinction in his letter to the disciples in Colossae. He exhorts them, *'See to it that no one takes you captive through philosophy and empty deception, according to the tradition of men, according to the elementary principles of the world, rather than according to Christ'* (Colossians 2:8).

In Jesus' Kingdom, we can no longer build our lives on the traditions or practices of men. We are to look to the commandments of God. By way of illustration, the story told in 2 Kings chapter 17 may help us here.

The people of Israel, at this time, were divided into the Northern Tribes and the Southern Kingdom of Judah. Both countries were led by weak and corrupt kings. Both countries were also falling back into the pagan practices of their neighbours and of the peoples who had originally lived in the land, walking in their customs and fearing their gods (v. 7–8). They set up for themselves sacred pillars and an Asherim (wooden symbol of a female deity) on top of the hills and under the trees, burning incense on all the high places and serving idols (v. 10–12). God warned both Israel and Judah, through the prophets, exhorting them to return to the godly traditions that had been given to their forefathers and to turn from their evil ways. But they did not listen, choosing to reject God's statutes in favour of those around them. They turned away from God's commandments by making idols for themselves, serving Baal and worshipping the heavenly bodies. They practised divination and were also involved in the casting of spells (v. 13–17). This was clearly against God's law as recorded in Deuteronomy 18:10–12:

> *'There shall not be found among you anyone who makes his son or daughter pass through the fire, one who uses divination, one who practices witchcraft, or one who interprets omens, or a sorcerer, or one who casts a spell, or a medium, or a spiritualist, or one who calls up the dead. For whoever does these things is detestable to the Lord.'*

God's judgement fell – Israel was defeated by the Assyrians and taken off into exile and the victorious invaders then sent an occupying force into Samaria, only to find themselves attacked by lions. Fearing for their lives, they hastily sent for help, asking a local priest to teach them the customs of Israel's God (v. 18–27). They did not want to displease Him! Eventually, the Assyrians ended up fearing the Lord, serving their own gods and following the ancient practices and traditions of the pagans. What a mess!

We are God's people of today, a people for His own possession, but are we in a similar predicament? Do we fear and trust the Lord, while also following the religious traditions and superstitions of our pagan ancestors? We may even believe, to some extent, in an element of good fortune, local 'knowledge' or fate. 'Religious', in this context, is not a substitute for the commandments of God. **Jesus came to set us free from the religious traditions of men that will inevitably deny the power of God, even if they do masquerade as 'godly' or 'Christian'** (2 Timothy 3:5).

For example, our pagan ancestors would have originally celebrated the Ancient Rites of spring with fertility rituals. However, in an attempt to counteract the pagan influence, our Christian predecessors turned these into the religious Easter celebrations. The point is that both follow the traditions of men and not the commandments of God. Every year, the date of Easter is actually fixed according to the phase of the moon. According to the traditions of men, this is when we are to remember the death and celebrate the resurrection of Jesus. The traditions of God, however, instruct us to do this whenever we renew covenant with each other in the sharing out of bread and wine (1 Corinthians 11:26). In our generation, it is significant that the religious veneer, reminiscent of the shiny paper on an Easter egg, is wearing thin, revealing the true nature of the festival.

According to a similar pagan philosophy, Christmas is celebrated around the time of the mid-winter solstice and there have been many traditions of men built up around this time of the year. These are in marked contrast to biblical revelation or instruction. Nowhere in the Bible are we encouraged to give Jesus a birthday, and even if we were, most scholars would agree that this would almost certainly not be in December. Again, the days of tinsel, cribs and angelic hosts are numbered. Angels are currently 'descending' in favour of the ancient and astrological symbols that portray the likeness of the sun, moon and stars. These are, quite literally, in ascendance, and reflect the ethos of our society. Deuteronomy 4:19 warns us:

> *'And beware, lest you lift up your eyes to heaven and see the sun and the moon and the stars, all the host of*

heaven, and be drawn away and worship them and serve them, those which the Lord your God has allotted to all the peoples under the whole heaven.'

As Christians, we should no longer feel pressurized to observe these religious traditions. We are not to become enslaved by them (Galations 4:9–10); nor should we begin to judge each other on their account (Colossians 2:16; Romans 14:1–6).

According to the traditions of men, we are living on the brink of the 'Age of Aquarius', symbolizing the pouring in of a new spirit in a New Age. People in our generation are genuinely searching for new spiritual truth and they are quite prepared to go outside God's mandate to find it.

Many people look to the stars, or to fortune telling, for revelation of their destiny. Some seek a higher 'consciousness' beyond the realms of reality, aspiring to levels of awareness leading to the ever-elusive state of 'enlightenment'. For others, life is in the 'lap of the gods' and they resign themselves to a life of passivity. Life, for them, is a predetermined fate controlled by some dominant, capricious energy force. The concept of death has also been mellowed with the soothing philosophies of reincarnation. This may be one reason for the added zeal in the advocation of animal rights and vegetarianism. In some philosophies, 'God' is purported to be in every living thing and a human life is subsequently regarded as having no more intrinsic value than any other animal. In others, God is no longer in the equation at all and we are just another species, a product of nature with no eternal significance.

As disciples in Jesus' Kingdom, how does the spirit of the age influence us? Are you personally affected? For example, it may seem laudable to 'save the planet', but we can easily be deceived into thinking that we are addressing purely issues of our generation. We may think that the Green Movement is a new campaign. However, though it has a lot to commend it, much of its underlying philosophy is unbiblical. It has actually grown out of an ancient worship and belief in 'mother earth' as the source and sustainer of life. This contradicts the worship of Father God who has put Jesus at His right hand and is upholding everything by the word of His power (Hebrews 1:3). Psalm 102:25–27 tells us that the heavens and earth actually **will** wear out like an old garment and that He will change them. But God Himself will never change and His years will never end.

Obviously, we need to live responsibly, taking care of the creation that God has given us (Genesis 1:28–31). However, we may be living our lives worrying or giving up a disproportional amount of time and energy in supporting causes to prolong the life of our planet. If so, then we may need to question our own priorities and basic insecurity.

As Christians, we are not immune from the opinions of the world around us. At this present time, even our friends and neighbours are returning to the 'old remedies' and commending to us the old pagan traditions and superstitions. Sometimes these may be in the guise of 'alternative medicine'. **These philosophies may have been revamped to suit the current climate, but their origins are usually ungodly**. Most often, their founders have either been firmly rooted in the occult or they have followed humanistic or religious world views that are in direct opposition to biblical teachings. In short, they are usually founded upon superstition and the religious traditions of men rather than the commandments of God. Each branch of alternative medicine will obviously have to be judged according to its own merit.

Many remedies involve the services of a 'spiritual healer'. This person is called upon to interpret the nature of the problem or even to charm it away. Even if the diagnosis and treatment bring forth seemingly good results, it is tapping into the wrong source (Deuteronomy 18:11). Being a spiritual healer, in this sense, is definitely not a gift of the Holy Spirit as portrayed in 1 Corinthians chapter 12. Spiritual healing is a counterfeit gift that does not acknowledge Jesus as Lord (1 Corinthians 12:3). In addition, other supernatural giftings that are clearly counterfeit or outside God's mandate include: telepathy, clairvoyance, astral-projection, levitation, fortune-telling, wart charming, divination or any other kind of magic.

The Bible teaches that even false prophets can perform great signs and miracles to deceive (Matthew 24:24). Even Satan himself can masquerade as an angel of light (2 Corinthians 11:14).

We need to understand that New Age is, quite literally, as old as the hills and that it is walking outside God's commandments. On the surface, many New Age aspirations are credible, even commendable. **People get sucked in by their natural curiosity or a genuine desire to find God, but they invite temptation and compromise. They also court demonic involvement in their lives** (1 Timothy 4:1).

Our own parents or grandparents may have been involved in aspects of pagan worship. These may have included: astrology, spiritualism, witchcraft or free-masonry. Where their sins have influenced us, we need to repent and be set free (Nehemiah 1:6). Where we have dabbled, the same principle will apply.

Let's now pick up the story of Israel and Judah again. 2 Kings chapter 18 tells us that, in contrast to the Northern Tribe of Israel, Judah returned to the commandments of God. Hezekiah (the new king) *'did right in the sight of the Lord, according to all that his father David had done'* (v. 3). Take note of what he did:

> *'He removed the high places and broke down the sacred pillars and cut down the Asherah. He also broke in pieces the bronze serpent that Moses had made, for until those days the sons of Israel burned incense to it; and it was called Nehushtan.'*   (2 Kings 18:4)

Hezekiah was radical. He removed the old pagan influences that remained in Judah. He tore down the Asherah or family idols (as did Gideon in Judges 6:25) and he put a stop to religious rituals.

The bronze serpent which Hezekiah broke in pieces was the same one that Moses had lifted up in the wilderness. This was for the Israelites to look at when they were bitten during the plague of poisonous snakes. As the Israelites looked at the bronze serpent, they were instantly healed (Numbers 21:8–9). Even Jesus referred to it, saying that He would be lifted up in the same way so that whoever believed in Him would have eternal life (John 3:14–15). For the Israelites, this sacred symbol had itself become an object of worship, and God was certainly not displeased with Hezekiah for destroying it. Could the same thing be said of the cross today?

Hezekiah, we are told, clung to the Lord, keeping the commandments which God had previously given to Moses (2 Kings 18:6). In clinging to the traditions of God, he also tore down the traditions of men where these had centred on idolatry or had turned into religious rituals. God was pleased with Hezekiah and caused him to prosper wherever he went (v. 7). Following their radical repentance, God even fought on Judah's behalf. When they were in battle with the King of Assyria, He sent an angel into the Assyrian camp during the night, killing one hundred and eighty-five thousand of their men. **God chose to bless Hezekiah and the Kingdom of Judah because they chose to obey His commandments, and we would be wise to follow their example.**

We may have pride in a 'Christian Country'. This may be symbolized by flag-waving or the keeping of patriotic days such as St George's, Thanksgiving or Independence. We may take pride in the ritualistic mystique of the Coronation ceremony. But could these ever be used to form a patriotic religious veil disguising the true colours of nationalism, racism and pride? God wants to bless our country in the same way as He wants to bless us. Jesus taught that His Kingdom was not of this world (John

18:36). His blessings will follow wherever loyalty and allegiance is given to Him.

Whether we are flag-waving or not, it is interesting that many traditions of men, especially those of a religious nature, focus on the externals but never quite get to the heart of the matter. For example, some of our behaviour at funerals can be bizarre. We may feel ourselves obliged to wear black. We speak in hushed tones as if there was a danger of waking the person lying dead in the coffin! This may give the appearance of solemnity and respect but could actually mask a fear of death itself. For those of us who are disciples of Jesus, death no longer holds any fear (Hebrews 2:14–15). It could even be said that it holds a certain excitement as we look forward to our eternal inheritance that is kept for us in heaven (1 Peter 1:4). There will be understandable heartache for those who have been separated from their loved ones, but even in the midst of grieving, it is always fitting to praise God.

Jesus had a lot to say about the kind of traditions that give the appearance of respectability (Matthew 6:1–6). If we are going to church wearing our 'Sunday best', to give a false impression of ourselves, we will need to repent! Jesus has come to set us free in these things, because God looks upon the heart and is not fooled by our outward appearance (1 Samuel 16:7). When we read the Gospels, Jesus was neither meek nor mild when addressing these issues. He despised any kind of hypocrisy in those around him:

> *'Woe to you, scribes and Pharisees, hypocrites! For you clean the outside of the cup and of the dish, but inside they are full of robbery and self-indulgence. You blind Pharisee, first clean the inside of the cup and of the dish, so that the outside of it may become clean also. Woe to you, scribes and Pharisees, hypocrites! For you are like whitewashed tombs which on the outside appear beautiful, but inside they are full of dead men's bones*

and all uncleanness. Even so, you too outwardly appear righteous to men, but inwardly you are full of hypocrisy and lawlessness.' (Matthew 23:25–28)

God looks at the attitudes of our hearts and not external appearances (1 Samuel 16:7; Galatians 5:6). If we are genuinely seeking to live righteously before Him, then this will bring us enormous freedom (Galatians 5:1).

Fully understanding how our religious traditions have evolved may seem complex, yet the principles shown by God in feeding the children of Israel in the wilderness are most important here. God provided for His people daily, sending them manna that was found on the ground as the morning dew evaporated (Exodus 16:14). This manna was like coriander seed, tasting like wafers with honey (v. 31) but could not be kept for storage unless in specific response to God's command (v. 24). If the provision was kept, it quickly became contaminated with worms (v. 20), becoming stale and worthless.

The Israelites were daily dependent upon God for their provision and God's heart is the same for us. Any God-given provision of today, even if initiated by the Holy Spirit, can rapidly turn into a ritualistic tradition of tomorrow, becoming stale and lifeless to all who take part. God's love to us is new every morning (Lamentations 3:22–23). We are to live in *'newness of the Spirit'* rather than *'oldness of the letter'* (Romans 7:6).

In summary, it may be helpful to reiterate what the Bible teaches about religious practices. Firstly, God calls for loyalty and allegiance from His people – we are not to follow the religious practices of pagans. Secondly, the Bible calls for diligence so that we do not slip back into our old ways, but walk according to the Spirit rather than according to the flesh (Galatians 3:3). Thirdly, the Bible warns us not to follow new religions (Deuteronomy 6:14; Colossians 2:8; 2 Timothy 4:3–4).

An 'all embracing' kind of attitude pervades our society today, but the philosophy behind it is not in line with the teachings of the Bible. Jesus said,

> *'Enter by the narrow gate; for the gate is wide, and the way is broad that leads to destruction, and many are those who enter by it. For the gate is small, and the way is narrow that leads to life, and few are those who find it.'* (Matthew 7:13–14)

The religious traditions and superstitions of our generation may be very beguiling. If we feel affectionately drawn towards them, as this lady found, Jesus can most definitely set us free:

> 'God showed me that there was something "latent" inside me – something that was in existence although I hadn't actively developed it. It was influencing me. I would find myself half-heartedly defending certain other philosophies. I used to find it hard to conceive that other beliefs were wrong and that only Christians were right. Wasn't this arrogance? In my heart, I perceived Jesus as rather narrow-minded; surely there were other paths to God? It was as if there were two sides to me. I was convinced beyond doubt that Jesus was real and knew that God had dealt radically in my life. I was convinced that I knew His voice. But there was this other part of me; an unhealthy affection towards other philosophies that couldn't be explained. I knew I needed to repent.
>
> Since repenting, something inside has changed. I don't understand exactly how, but I know that God has set me free and there is no longer any empathy with other beliefs or philosophies. There is nothing in my heart that warms to them. In fact, in my life I now want to expose false religion and help set people free.'

Jesus said:

> *'I am the way, and the truth, and the life; no one comes to the Father, but through Me.'* (John 14:6)

As a disciple, do you agree?

By way of illustration, we have included the following testimonies. If you are enslaved by any religious tradition or superstition, Jesus can set you free.

Easter

'I have been a Christian since I was eleven but realize now how religious I used to be. For example, I used to take Lent very seriously, denying myself the most ridiculous of things. My motivation was that I wanted to please God, but I had never realized that this was actually a "dead work" that had not been initiated by the Holy Spirit. On Good Fridays, I did not feel free to be frivolous or to enjoy myself in a light-hearted way although this had not been forced upon me; my parents were not even church-goers. Similarly, on Easter Sunday, I would love to get up at daybreak and attend the earliest church service – somehow it seemed more holy! I wanted to show Jesus that He was worth the effort of getting out of bed. Although this was not wrong in itself, the reality of Jesus being alive is not confined to one day or to a season. It's worth celebrating every day!'

Christmas

'I had a friend who had taken a personal stand against the tide. Years ago, he had given Christmas and all its associated trappings the left boot of fellowship! Christmas, he pointed out, was at its root a pagan festival that had been hijacked by Christians. Biblically, there is no instruction (or hint) that we should celebrate the birth of the Saviour of the world. In fact, the opposite is true! We celebrate his death in the breaking of bread. I wondered at the time whether this was a reaction to his brethren upbringing, or a truly radical challenge to the status quo. However, his gracious yet firm stance, was a source of real inspiration to me.

Over the years, as I embraced a more radical approach to church life, Christmas became a big issue. Should I continue with a religious and national tradition that had no scriptural warrant? Despite the protestations of my fellow evangelical friends, was Christmas really a "good time of the year" for outreach? I had, personally, seen very little fruit in the many Christmas outreaches I had been involved in. What would be the effects on my family and friends if I ditched this "holy tradition"? For some, it would appear that I was committing heresy!

I read again the paper that my friend had written years earlier on the roots of Christmas. I needed no further prompting and was convinced. To perpetuate Christmas was unhelpful to the process of "setting the captives free". The apostle Paul made it clear to the Galatians that he considered the observation of days, months, seasons and years as *'weak and worthless elemental things'* that enslave the believer (Galatians 4:9–10). He said, *'It was for freedom that Christ set us free; therefore keep standing firm and do not be subject again to a yoke of slavery'* (Galations 5:1).

I could see that to load on my own young family obligations of a religious festival could interfere with their own radical pursuit of God in the future. The commitments to presents, cards and decorations had to go. So did the sentimental but not necessarily heartfelt wishes for the coming new year. We talked the issues through with our children and wrote to family and friends explaining our actions and releasing them from any obligation to send cards, presents, etc.

I can only say that the response was amazing. My non-Christian friends were more understanding than some Christian ones! I have not been called Scrooge once! Not celebrating Christmas has opened up many more opportunities to share with unbelievers the good news that Jesus came to set us free from these things. Our children do not feel left out or "weird" at school. We have encouraged them to come to their own convictions.

We are financially better off. We give presents and gifts when God tells us, not because we are obliged to. Walking down the high street in December and feeling no "pull" to partake of the Christmas buying spree is wonderful! The sentimentality of Christmas trees, lights and small dollies in cribs has no pull on our emotions. But more than all the practical benefits, is the joy of knowing the real freedom in Christ our decision has made.'

Sundays

'My parents loved me, accepted me and made me feel totally secure in the family home but one thing I could never understand was why Sundays were such a big deal. The world seemed to stop on a Sunday because this was the "Lord's Day". We didn't go to the beach, play outside, go shopping, watch television, knit or even hang out the washing. My clothes were Sunday best. Everything about Sundays was different.

My parents were Christians and really loved God, but I couldn't understand their legalism about this one day because there were so many dos and don'ts. I dreaded Sunday coming. In fact, I hated Sundays!

As I grew up, I drifted away from God, never having really found a relationship with Him for myself. A few years later, however, God broke in on me in a powerful way. Despite this, I still found it very difficult to shake off the family's "Sunday tradition". Going to the beach on Sundays somehow seemed like letting God down and going to the shop still felt as if it was a terrible witness for a Christian. Although I tried, I still couldn't seem to shake off this religious tradition, even though I hated it.

One day, in a ministry time, I finally saw it for what it really was: religiosity, tradition and hypocrisy. If things appeared religious on the surface, that was all that had mattered. This attitude had actually been rooted in my family for generations and was tied up with spiritual pride.

What a difference to be free to be myself, knowing that God wants a relationship with me all the time. He is interested in my heart and not what I do on the outside for others to see.'

Transcendental Meditation

'I read about Transcendental Meditation in a cafe. It promised happiness, health, longevity and peace of mind. Perfect!

I rang up, paid my £50 fee and was greeted by love and harmony; special people. Instantly, I fell in the trap and all discernment went from me because I was desperate to feel loved again. They told me to bring some items, a new white handkerchief, fruit or flowers. I was eager to start the course. All week they had been asking me questions about my beliefs, my home life and even politics. They performed their ceremony, asking me to bow down in front of a photo of Maharishi. Then they gave me my mantra and told me never to share it.

To begin with I felt at peace, even happy, but soon I began to get very obsessive about TM. What had started out as ten to twenty minutes of meditation sometimes resulted in two to three hours. Several times I remember my heart slowing down and feeling everything was so peaceful I just wanted to let go. I became more spiritually sensitive and felt presences in my room. Sometimes they felt like friends, sometimes a little menacing.

I went to a TM relaxation weekend where they had a very strict timetable. There was meditation, yoga, breathing exercises and videos of how TM worked. We ate vegetarian foods and in the evening, someone would play a tape of the Yogis chanting. Then, in silence, we all had to go to our rooms.

After the weekend, we went home. I was encouraged not to watch television, read the newspapers or listen to music so that I could reach a higher level of awareness. I was still meditating regularly but was also depressed, lonely and hurt. The only way I could escape was by cutting myself off from reality and reaching enlightenment. I saw illuminated colours – blobs of green and purple enveloping me in my mind's eye. Reaching other levels of awareness was all that I wanted to achieve.

Despite all this, my life did not change. I had just the same hurt feelings and hang-ups but they were disguised by being detached. I started to put my family and my friends under pressure about TM for themselves.

After four years, I was still as emotionally screwed up as when I had begun.

I started getting into spiritual healing and New Age spiritualism. These people seemed the only ones who understood my needs. They told me that I was very special, with gifts that needed to be developed and that they would help me. They said I was different, that I had a very old soul whereas my husband had a very young one. Mediums, clairvoyants and gypsies all had the same message for me.

I started having spiritual attacks. Bad premonitions and horrific nightmares led me to see healers each week. They assured me that they were getting rid of these negative energies around me. I was also taught methods of how to close down my channels when I needed to. Every night, I went through these rituals to protect myself but they didn't help. Every day I felt frightening spiritual forces closing in on me. I was too scared to be on my own.

Soon after this, I had a physical attack. This time, I was desperate to find the right help. At 11.30 pm on a Saturday night, my husband and I searched for a vicar. It felt as if there were a vacuum of energy on my head and as if I were levitating. I was terrified and I called out to God, but my gods had been very varied (from Krishna to Buddha). I did not know to call out to Jesus. That night we found a vicar. He prayed in the name of Jesus and commanded the spirit to go, which it did.

That night was the beginning of a genuine encounter with God that changed my life. After experiencing the very real power of Jesus, I knew which way to go. I made a decision to put all other false religions behind me. In Jesus, I am at last finding the love and acceptance I had been longing for. He has forgiven me for my past life and it is such a relief to know that I have been adopted into His family. Now, I can stop searching. At last, I belong.'

Astral-Projection

'A close friend of mine was confessing how he had been involved in transcendental meditation and astral-projection. I knew a bit about the first so was able to look vaguely intelligent and nod in the right places, but I had simply never heard of astral-projection. As we spoke, I shifted uncomfortably in my chair.

He described how he had trained himself to wake up while dreaming. If he was lucky, he could experience flying. Had he not given up, it would have been possible for him to float on the ceiling, to transport himself and also to levitate. I was shocked at what he was talking about. I had been able to do most of these things ever since I could remember!

I stumbled out of the house and drove home in a daze. Panic awoke me in the night. "What are you doing?" asked my wife. "Putting some clothes on," I replied. "I thought I was going out of the window just now." I didn't want to find myself outside at 3.00 am with no clothes on, knocking at the door to get back in!

I realized that I could fly in my dreams and float on the ceiling. As a child, I would constantly sleep walk, sometimes waking to find myself anywhere in the house.

Where did this come from? I began to see it was obviously not from God. In fact, God wanted to free me from my nights of troubled sleep! For years, I had experienced a recurring dream where I was running away as if I were afraid of something but never knowing what. I felt that, if I were actually caught, I would somehow be found guilty of something.

As I repented of my astral-projection, I experienced the power of God breaking in on my situation. I knew that I had been set free from fear and guilt. Praise God for my freedom! I now enjoy a good night's sleep! My recurring dream is long past, and since my repentance, I have never been disturbed by strange phenomena.'

Homeopathy

'A subtle lie that the enemy uses is the premise that anything that produces seemingly "good" results must itself be originating from good.

I had been a Christian for some years and would not knowingly have got involved in anything that was obviously evil. However, because I was dissatisfied with conventional medicine and impatient for God to act in my own life, I became involved in Ictheopathy (a branch of Homeopathy). At first, I was a patient and then later became a practitioner. I even started to see the business as God's provision for my financial needs. I had indeed bought into the lie – "hook, line and sinker!"

The results were good, especially for animal patients. Being valued by my clients fed a need in me to be wanted. However, after some time, a leader of our church challenged me on the origins of a variety of alternative medicines and Homeopathy in particular. At that point, I had no revelation on the issue myself, but told God that I was willing to be obedient to the leadership of the church.

There were consequences that had to be faced following the decision to close down my business. Several people telephoned and tried to persuade me to take on more consultancies – they would pay any fee I named. There was no question of going back on my promise to God. He proved to me that He is indeed no man's debtor. A friend of the family gave us a paid holiday to Florida as an impromptu gift – that sort of thing had never happened to us before!

However, ceasing to practise something that was wrong didn't get me totally free from its effects. A few weeks later, I responded to a word that was brought in a church meeting and after being prayed for, was finally freed from the spirits of infirmity and fear of death. God gave me a picture of a poisonous rat that had infected many areas of my life. Until that point, I had not seen it for what it was. With the deliverance came revelation. Suddenly, I was really motivated to sever every connection with New Age. I burnt many expensive books and more freedom came with their destruction. We changed our telephone number and then subsequently moved house. I am totally convinced that no cost was too great for the freedom achieved.'

Special Gifting

'I have always had a deep rooted sense of knowing that I was "special". This opened me up to receive and then subsequently use, a "special gifting". I found that I had a natural leaning towards most things that required intuitive skills beyond the natural.

After being introduced to alternative medicine by a friend, I quickly picked up the technique required to practice Applied Kinesiology. I found it hard to understand why so many people who trained in this branch of alternative medicine were unable to use the technique with the same ease as I experienced.

As someone who had been a Christian for many years, it came as an enormous shock to me to discover that this "special gifting" was quite definitely not from God.'

External Religion

'For years, I never realized how bound I was in external religious things. They made me feel good but it was nothing to do with being a disciple. I loved the traditions of the church and all the priests in their garments and I adored the church building with all its statues. I often prayed to the statues of Mary and Jesus and always sat in my own place. Before I could sit, I felt that I had to bow down before the crucifix and "cross" myself. I couldn't ever do anything like laugh in church and was scared stiff at funerals. I prayed for the dead, lighting and kissing a candle for the person who had died. Around my neck, I wore a crucifix. I felt it protected me and many people kissed it. I idolized my parish priest, even though he was a homosexual and always did what he told me to do. It never even crossed my mind that some of the teaching was wrong. Much of the time, I was driven by fear.

At my twenty-fifth wedding anniversary, I had my marriage blessed. It was a big ceremony with a few priests there. I loved every minute of it. Now I realize that it was so religious and didn't do my marriage any good at all.

As I am seeing the issues, Jesus is setting me free from all this external religiosity.'

Chapter 6

Familiar People

The word 'familiar' reflects a variety of meanings in the English language. In this chapter, we would like to look behind the relationships we have with the 'familiar people' in our lives.

The Bible has much to say about how we should relate to fellow members of our local church. We are to be controlled by Christ's love; not making judgements according to the flesh, because God has made us into new creations. We have been born again of the Spirit. No longer are we to recognize each other according to how we were before we knew God, because Jesus has already paid the price for our past lives. We are now reconciled to Him (2 Corinthians 5:14–21).

If we are not to regard each other *'according to the flesh'*, then how are we to relate? Jesus said that we are not to judge each other according to appearances but according to righteous judgement (John 7:24). Let's not be like the scribes and Pharisees who judged by the wrong criterion! (John 8:15). We are to be controlled by love, making no judgements according to worldly standards.

The good news of the Gospel is that when the Kingdom is embraced, walls of prejudice are broken down. We are to show no partiality for a Jew or Greek, an American, African, or Asian! We are not to judge each other according to social status, class or education. The Kingdom of

God cuts across all bigotries of race, colour, social status, and gender (Galatians 3:28).

Whatever our colour, race or class in society, it is all too easy to evaluate others from an egocentric standpoint, assuming that we are the yardstick by which normality is to be measured. This is a very proud stance to maintain. It will eventually spill over into the church, affecting our sharing of lives together. As in the following example, God may use very mundane circumstances to teach us:

'We had been away for the weekend with some people from our church and had been praying and waiting on God for most of the day. Around early evening, we broke for a meal. I was really hungry. Halfway through eating, it was remarked upon how my husband and I were "posh", in a rather derogatory way. Maybe it was something to do with the way we were eating – I really don't remember. It set my mind racing. "Fair enough," I thought, "we may seem posh to you but this really isn't the issue." "So what is the opposite to posh?" I asked, thinking that my leading question would result in a fit of giggling and the holding up of the white flag. "Normal," he replied. He really was serious! I over-reacted. What pride!

Later, I needed to repent of my own reaction, but it illustrated to me how it is possible to inadvertently hold ourselves up as the centre of reference. We all do it!

I had originally grown up in a small town and then subsequently spent some time away, mixing with people from several different classes and cultures. In that environment, there had been many occasions where I had felt anything but posh! My own experience was painfully limited – there's a great big world out there!'

In your heart, do you really desire to be controlled by the love of Christ in your relationships? Do you really want to treat each person as you would wish to be treated (Luke 6:31)? **If you do, then part of the lifelong process of change will be the laying down of your personal bigotries, your preconceived ideas and biases.**

The Bible teaches that we are not to be unjust in our judgements of each other. We are not to be *'partial to the poor'*, nor are we *'to defer to the great'* (Leviticus 19:15). Sometimes, however, even if we have determined to 'put off the old' and 'put on the new', some circumstances may bring our old preconceptions to the light. Consider this next illustration:

'We three were the "lads", about twenty years old, living in a student flat. The only thing we had in common was Jesus. Each of us had a testimony of God's hand on our lives and enjoyed sharing it with others. We were friends, our divergent class backgrounds making no difference.

One evening, for fun, we set off to explore a little local history on our doorstep. After following a map and asking passers-by, we tracked down the site of the largest single mining disaster in the North East. The mine had long since closed; the slag heap gone. The only remaining evidence was a stone memorial in the little churchyard among the nettles. We approached this in the fading dusk. There were scores of names carved into the granite – all ages, boys and girls under ten to men in their eighties.

As we walked back, our conversation restarted. How had so many died? Why were two whole shifts trapped? It was, as with many such tragedies, down to money in the end. Lives were cheaper then.

Back in the flat, conversation became more heated when just like a spark into gun powder, my friends were at each other, struggling, fighting and shouting abuse. "You upper class snob!" one said. "You ignorant peasant," said the other. They grappled and as I tried to force them apart, I found myself "piggy-in-the-middle" in more ways than one! "You middle class are so complacent – you know nothing!" They turned on me in fury!

The arguments raged and deep resentments poured out, old and new. Finally, things calmed down.

Relationships were patched up but we really did not know what to do with the stuff and the things said. I guess we put it down to "just one of those things". Nevertheless, deep down, I realized that deeper issues belied the minor irritating habits we had previously seen in each other.'

Whatever the nature of these deeper issues, take the opportunity to deal with your inner bigotries as they reveal themselves. God's purpose is that you become more like Jesus. We are to *'dispense true justice'* (Zechariah 7:9), practising kindness and compassion to each other. Sometimes, it is difficult to understand all our preferences and antagonisms. In these circumstances, we are completely dependent upon God to reveal the root of our reactions. This was certainly the case in the following saga!

'I had always felt a "draw" to Americans. There was something I found almost irresistible about them. I had always desperately wanted an American friend.

A new family had started to attend our meetings and the lady was American. I felt compelled, almost, to befriend her. She seemed very aloof and defensive, yet I, for some reason, persevered in the building of this relationship I had always sought.

Over some time, a good relationship had developed and yet there were still reactions and comments from my friend that puzzled and often hurt me.

At a meeting one evening, I knew that God was stirring something inside. In my head, I could see a film running. I could hear the noises, smell the smells and even feel the atmosphere. I recognized where I was; I was in a bleak location of Scotland and there were lots of people around in very old fashioned dress. Among other things, there was chanting and strange noises of bagpipes. I was reminded of my Scottish descent, which had never been important to me before. I asked God if there was something in this to be sorted out. It was all so bizarre – what had my Scottish heritage to do with me now?

The next day, I felt prompted to look for the history of my Scottish connections. I came across a baby record book and as I flicked through it, I saw a page of my family tree. I was just looking at my link into the Clan, when in my mind, I saw something superimposed on top of it. It was a name. As I looked at it, I realized that I had seen it before somewhere – it was my American friend's signature, her maiden name that I had seen in the front of her Bible.

A few days later, I started to explain to my American friend about the Scottish film I had seen while being prayed for. She became very agitated and asked me to stop. I jokingly said to her, "Ah, but there's more..." and went on to explain about the handwriting. My friend felt sick and said that her "insides" felt as if they were "jumping through the roof!"

Over the next few weeks, we discovered that we were of the same generation of the same Clan; my side of the Clan stayed in Scotland and my friend's side went to America.

One night, while we were together with other friends, seeking God about the "Scottish saga", I again saw a "film". This time it was of a girl standing at a harbour, watching an old tall ship sailing away. What was prevalent, over everything else, was the emotion I felt; such intense unhappiness and isolation. I knew God was showing me the Clan separation. It was causing such pain for those left behind and terrible anger and resentment in those going away. Both my friend and I recognized the root of our reactions. I saw the root of my "draw" to her and she the root of her anger and jealousy towards me. In the spiritual realm, we were at war!

Over the following months, we were set free, sometimes painfully. We dealt with the past and all the unresolved conflicts of our forefathers. It became clear to us that spiritual forces in generations gone by had been outworking in us.

I sometimes reflect over this period and still find it so bizarre and unbelievable ... it could only have been God that helped us see the issues!'

One hallmark of a healthy Christian church are the varied backgrounds of its members. There will be people who have decided to join with those of different nationalities and social classes because of their common faith in Jesus. Within the church, however, if we only gravitate towards those of similar age, hobbies, intellect or social class, then a process of natural selection is taking place. We are recognizing each other according to the flesh.

Paul told Timothy to maintain principles within the church without bias, doing nothing in a spirit of partiality (1 Timothy 5:21). Again, the letter of James warns us not to hold our faith with an attitude of personal favouritism, making a distinction between those who are rich and those who have nothing. If we do show this kind of partiality, we are actually committing sin because we have become judges with evil motives. Even if someone is poor in this world, we do not judge them by this criterion. If they love God, they may be rich in faith, being heirs of the Kingdom (James 2:1–9).

In Acts chapter 10, God graciously showed Peter, through a vision, that the Gospel was available to all men irrespective of lineage or upbringing. God is not racist. *'In every nation the man who fears Him and does what is right, is welcome to Him'* (Acts 10:35).

If we are to show no partiality towards each other within the Church, this will set us free in the area of our friendships. Our affinity for each other will not be on a human level; it will be based upon our common experience of God and His goodness toward us. We are to imitate each other only as far as we see Jesus reflected (1 Corinthians 11:1). This will be the basis of our similarity. It is quite legitimate, in this sense, to be 'kindred spirits' with each other, just as Paul was with Timothy (Philippians 2:20). Since we all have the Holy Spirit in common there will be a God-given affinity between us. We are kinsmen, because God is our Heavenly Father. If there is any fellowship of the Spirit, we are to be of *'the same mind, maintaining the same love, united in spirit, intent on one purpose'* (Philippians 2:2).

Sometimes, God may join us with particular individuals who are 'special' people in our lives. These people may also be thought of as 'kindred spirits' or 'lifejoints of supply', facilitating the blessings of God to us by way of encouragement, revelation or ministry.

Each of us, deep inside, wants to be a 'special' person and we all have special people whom we call friends. Between friends there is a natural, healthy bonding of love and trust. Beyond this, some people have feelings of 'special bondings' with 'special people' that seem to others quite irrational and bizarre. They are able to communicate with each other over the miles as if by telepathy. Between them they have an unspoken loyalty and understanding. They may know instinctively, for example, if the other is in danger or ill.

Unless God has given a specific prophetic word or feeling at a specific time for a specific purpose, this kind of link with a particular individual is tapping into the wrong source. It is one of those practices forbidden by God (Deuteronomy 18:10–12). Evidently, it is possible to have a 'kindred spirit' that is not God-given.

For some, there may be certain people with whom they

make an instant 'connection', giving a feeling of spiritual unity. For example:

> 'I used to experience something that passed between me and certain other people. Maybe walking down the street, or in a room, there was a certain affinity or understanding; something in them was acknowledging something in me. I did not quite sit comfortably with it.
>
> One day, I was walking along the cliffs and came across a family walking the other way. Something uncanny passed between me and the other guy. He was sitting on a seat that I often sat on. There seemed a level of understanding that there should not have been – something very old and timeless – as if this had happened sometime before.
>
> A few weeks earlier, I was walking down the town and met a lady in the doorway of a shop. We got talking and she told me that she had been a "seeker" all her life. She had been involved in Hinduism and had also been to stay on a camp with Buddhist monks. We got on really well!
>
> Months before, God had clearly spoken to me in a meeting that I had been influenced by Hinduism. Now, something in me was responding to something in this lady.
>
> I was very open – sharing about Jesus and what He had done in my life. Then I gave her my address. A few days later, she turned up on my doorstep, still seeking. I shared the Gospel with her again but her response was that she thought I was a very "old soul" whereas she was a very "new one".
>
> God was certainly highlighting that this needed dealing with in my life!'

If we do make these 'connections' with people, we can easily be blinded to their significance until the Holy Spirit reveals the basis of our experience. These kind of feelings can run very deep and although they may operate at a subconscious level, they will inevitably affect our behaviour and attitudes. We may 'identify' with certain types of people. Consider this lady's attitude:

> 'One day, as I was being prayed for, God showed me how strongly I felt about the injustice of the American Indians being disturbed and how their way of life had been curtailed by the pioneers. What had really never crossed my mind before was that the Indians had worshipped countless pagan gods and were into the elements and the occult in a big way. I had always seen them as the innocent party, and wanted them to win in the cowboy films because the cowboys were always so insensitive and arrogant.
>
> That the attitude of the pioneers was both morally and politically unjust was not in question. For myself, however, I realized that something very deep inside me was responding to this "elemental" group of people. I was defending their causes and beliefs and thinking of them as spiritually sensitive and misunderstood.
>
> It slowly dawned upon me that, although we live in a totally different kind of environment, these types of people were still very attractive to me. As a Christian, I would never be drawn to anyone who was blatantly in direct opposition to the Gospel – but I was drawn towards "seekers". They had an air of mystery and knowledge, just like the Indians. They seemed such sensitive, understanding people. I could forgive them for anything so easily. There was a sense in which we "connected".'

Some people may find themselves actively drawn to those who dabble in the occult; this is not the work of the Holy Spirit! For example:

> 'I was once into much occult activity. That was before

I found what, or Who I was really searching for –
Jesus. I renounced and repented of all the occult
things I had been involved in. These included:
spiritualism, tarot cards, hand-readings, crystal ball,
vipassana meditation, séances, astrology, incense
sticks and drugs etc. In these practices I had really
opened myself up to demonic activity.

I was drawn to gypsies. If any happened to be in
town doing their thing, they always seemed to "home
in" on me. Even if I avoided them, I seemed to meet
another one who stopped me. I must confess that I
was drawn to them. I wanted to hear what they had
to foretell and it was hard to say "no".

Eventually, I was delivered from a familiar spirit.
Only a couple of days ago, the gypsies were in town
again. We walked straight past each other and I
turned to see them "home in" on another lady. I
don't feel drawn anymore. I am free and Jesus did it!'

God is working in each of us, bringing into the light
those things that have previously been hidden (Ephesians
5:13). In His church, His will is for us to walk together in
fellowship of the **Holy Spirit**, *'being of the same mind,
maintaining the same love, united in spirit, intent on one
purpose'* (Philippians 2:2).

Chapter 7

Familiar Places

'Familiar places', as well as 'familiar people', can evoke varied feelings and emotions. These feelings can influence our long-term decisions concerning where on earth we are going to spend the rest of our days.

In the context of Jesus' words to His disciples saying, *'Go into all the world and preach the gospel'* (Mark 16:15), in this chapter, we would like to bring perspectives from our own localities into sharper focus. This may help clarify both our local and world-wide vision.

First, what makes a place familiar? Usually, familiarity comes by simply seeing the same streets, houses or countryside over and over again. From earliest childhood days, memories are created in each of us. We remember fondly where we first learnt to ride a bicycle, went to school, played on the swings or fell and grazed our knee. Times of major upheaval can also leave lasting impressions. They may link particular places with life-changing events, relationships, dreams or aspirations. Even the mention of a place, or hearing the familiar local accent of days gone by can bring all these memories flooding back, releasing in us great emotion. We realize then that there are places we like and places we dislike.

For some people, familiar places may evoke feelings of love and belonging, adding to their sense of identity and purpose in life. They may be happy to stay at home, content with the tried and tested. Others may like to travel the world, tasting all the different sights and sounds, the very idea of leaving home filling them with excitement and anticipation. What may be familiar and friendly to one person may be strange and hostile to another.

As with everything else, when we decide to follow Jesus and embrace His Kingdom, we can no longer take our natural inclinations for granted. God may require us to travel the world to live and work for Him. Alternatively, He may require us to stay in the same small village for the rest of our days. Whether the Holy Spirit is impressing on us to stay or go, the issue is that we are constantly to live our lives in an attitude of willingness to do His will.

It would be difficult to tease out all the factors involved in our choice of where to live. For example, our decision may be based on an accumulation of things such as job availability, a suitable church, family or natural preferences. However, the Bible tells us that where our treasure is, there will our hearts be also (Matthew 6:21). Jesus said that His Kingdom was not of this world (John 18:36). If we really are storing up treasures in heaven, then we will develop a healthy perspective on our natural attachment to any particular place.

God's intention is that the beauty of what He has made would help reveal His eternal power and divine nature (Romans 1:20). His creation tells of His glory (Psalm 19:1). Yet occasionally, the fine line between worshipping God and worshipping what He has created becomes blurred. God has made a beautiful world for us to enjoy, but He does not want us to be enslaved by it. Consider the following illustration:

> 'The last time I visited Switzerland, I just loved to be in and around the mountains. I would have to see them in the mornings to gauge the weather and to see how the day would be.
>
> On the return journey, while driving through a tunnel, I started to cry and felt as if I were leaving

home. At this time, I had no knowledge of what this could mean other than a deep affection for this country.

Two years later, I had an argument with my wife about our holiday destination as I wanted to return to Switzerland and visit the same area. However, we were not able to go on holiday there again until this year. Just before we left, I was stirred that I needed release from my unhealthy affection for the mountains.

While on the subsequent holiday, I was able to enjoy the mountains without any ties or compulsion. The return journey was also completely uneventful and there were no problems about leaving.

I now realize that I am free to enjoy the beauty of whatever God has created without feeling "driven" or enslaved.'

Jesus has set us free to enjoy our freedom wherever we may go. Yet despite this, we may have very set ideas concerning where we would like to be or where we would most feel at home. Whether we are 'town' or 'country' at heart, and whether we aspire to a council house or executive suite, true freedom comes when we are content to live in either (Philippians 4:11).

For some people, it may be important to live within the sound of Bow Bells or within the boundaries of a certain county, town or suburban area. For them, living in a certain locality seems to reflect a perceived worth or identity. For others, it may be important to live within reach of open countryside or sight and sound of the sea. Still others may feel constrained to be 'at one' with creation, being overly attached to the elements, even feeling restless when contact with them is denied. God wants to come and set us free from these restrictions. For example:

'"What a load of rubbish," I thought, "What will they think of next? This is totally over the top!" Just some thoughts (the polite ones) that went through my mind when I first heard mention of how we may worship the elements. Wrong!

As time went on, God started to remind me of my reactions to His creation. I remembered that, as a little girl, I used to talk to trees and plants and hills. I gave them names and to me they had personality and feelings. I dismissed this. All children do that, don't they?

Then God brought to mind how I felt when I moved away from my home town to a city at eighteen years of age. I coped really well for a week. Then I started feeling "shut in". If only I could just see the sea. After a couple more weeks of feeling restless, I grabbed two friends and went in search of Weston-Super-Mare, or should I say Weston-Super-Mud! We were all horrified when we arrived and saw a stretch of mud and far out on the horizon something that was supposed to be the sea. I was sure that they could be done under the Trade Descriptions Act for calling that sea and I can still remember the feeling of disappointment.

I gradually got used to city-living, as long as every few weeks I could go home to the sea. I now realize it was like getting a fix. I would drive down the motorway and the nearer I got to home, the more excited I would feel. I knew exactly at which point I would get my first glimpse of the sea and as I got closer to it, the adrenalin would start to pump. As I saw the view, I would take a deep breath in and relax. I was home. As soon as possible, often before unpacking, I would go out and walk along the beach or cliffs. Here, I could feel the wind in my hair. I would smell the fresh air and feel the tension seep away from me. Then sometimes I would pray as I walked and thank God for His wonderful creation.

A few years later, I married and my husband and I moved to Devon. One of his complaints about me in the early days of our marriage was that whenever he heard me talking about home, it didn't mean where we lived. As much as I tried, I could not stop doing it.

All this sounds innocent enough – walking on the beach, enjoying God's creation, coming back to my roots – but the implications were not innocent. As the Holy Spirit was convicting me, my eyes were being opened to the restriction this was causing in my life. What if God called us to the inner city or "the ends of the earth"? I could not go, I was tied here.

I got some prayer and God set me free. Now I am free to stay and free to go.'

Whether God wants you to stay or to go, continually seek your happiness and security in Him, rather than in people or places. As you do this, God will surely give you the desires of your heart to be walking in His plan and purpose. When we give ourselves to Him, committing our way in an attitude of trust, then God is more than able to bring this to pass (Psalm 37:4–5), releasing us to fulfil it.

For this family, it was clearly time to move on:

'I come from a very close extended family – nearly all my relatives still live in the same town and see each other most days.

When God started challenging my husband and I about moving away from my home town, I really found it difficult to cope with. Although I knew God had a call on my life, and I wanted to fulfil it, I hadn't even considered He may want me to move. Even those family members who had gone away to college or for jobs had all come back to settle.

God started showing me that maybe this wasn't right, that maybe there was a ungodly reason behind it. I didn't want to move away because, to me, there was nowhere quite like home.

I had some prayer, and while we were praying, God began highlighting the spiritual dynamics within me.

Ironically, these were seeking to keep me locked to the very place where I would never fulfil God's purposes for my life.

My deliverance was very traumatic as the demonic manifestations seemed in the very essence of my being. It actually felt as if I were giving birth. God was exposing the very nature of those issues that had held my family together in one place for so long; the issues that were keeping me locked into a particular mould. During prayer, having had children, I literally felt as if I were in labour. I had contractions, panted, went into the transition period and as God released me from the hold of these things in my life, I actually felt as if I had given birth.

Since this deliverance, we have, in fact, moved away from my home town and extended family. God has clearly shown us that this was part of His purpose for our lives, and we are really happy in our new home.'

For many of us, certain 'familiar places' may, over a period of time, come to hold an important place in our hearts. They become 'special places' to which we return, seeking a safe haven from the pressures of life. These may be quiet solitary places with tranquil streams or rivers, wild lonely moorlands, woods or hillsides, beaches or cliffs. They could also be the busy highstreets encapsulating the anonymity, distraction or escapism of city life. We may gravitate towards a certain place in the garden, a special room or even (like Christopher Robin) a place on the stairs where we like to sit.

Certain places may bring a sense of timelessness to our ever-changing circumstances, even seeming to be great sources of security in times of turmoil. They may provide a reference point and a sense of constancy or stability when other relationships have let us down. Here, we can feel truly alive and in touch with our senses; able to breathe again.

As time goes by, these well-loved familiar haunts may even become closer to us than a friend, sharing the most intimate details of our lives. This may seem reasonable enough, even desirable, but God has made it known that He wants to occupy first place in our hearts, giving us a feeling of security and solace. The Bible tells us that God is our refuge and God is our strength (Psalm 46:1–2). He is even our hiding place in times of trouble (Psalm 32:7).

> *'I look to the mountains; where will my help come from? My help will come from the Lord, who made heaven and earth.'* (Psalm 121:1–2 GNB)

Have you a certain place where you 'touch base', a place you would like to end your days or have your ashes scattered?
Consider this next testimony:

> 'I used to find a kind of heightened spiritual awareness at a certain place I used to go to, a sense of reverence and immortality. It was a place of personal solace. I used go there when I needed to be alone, sometimes sharing it with the special people in my life. Then, one day, as we were praying about something else, God revealed to me that I was actually "worshipping" this place. I would go into shops and my eyes would be scanning the postcard racks just to see if I could catch a glimpse of it. It made me feel at home and secure, giving a feeling of belonging. I even wrote poems about this place and mixed my thoughts up about how wonderful it was and how wonderful to find God there.
>
> What I had never realized was that this was idolatry – I was worshipping a place – I was worshipping something other than God.
>
> While I was being prayed for, there was a sobbing, "I love this place, I love this place." I shall never

forget the experience because it did not seem to be me that was initiating the speaking.

For a short while after this experience, I was not free to visit this place because I was very wary. I knew that the locality had held a place of great importance for generations in my family and I did not want this affection fostered in my own children. Now there is freedom to go there and enjoy a good day out because the place holds no emotional or spiritual significance for me. It is no longer home.'

Some people inwardly long to have this kind of particular place, a place where they can truly find their roots and feel 'at home'. For them, there is a basic insecurity or lack of identity. Who am I? Where have I come from? Where do I belong?

Many people go through life never really feeling as if they belong anywhere at all. They are continually searching for somewhere that will meet their needs. Again, God wants to be this place in our lives. His will is that His loved ones would dwell in the security of His protection (Deuteronomy 33:12). Here, under the shelter of His wings, we will find everything we have ever lacked (Psalm 91).

Having established that our real 'home' is in God and that it is in Him that we find our security, then what will be our heart towards the particular locality in which we actually do live? Most importantly, we will hold the place loosely while having a real heart for the people living within it.

Let's return to 2 Kings chapter 17 again, this time in the context of people and places.

Earlier, we saw that the powerful Assyrian army successfully invaded and conquered the northern tribes of Israel. Subsequently, the Babylonians went on to conquer the southern Kingdom of Judah. The victorious invaders then took the finest Israeli soldiers and noble families into exile, choosing to settle in the promised land themselves.

When the exiled Jews returned, about seventy years later, the foreign settlers were obviously very unpopular because they had taken over the Jewish houses, land and farms. Although they married into the local community, they were still considered impostors and foreigners. In time, however, they became segregated and formed a nation between the old northern Israel and the southern Kingdom of Judah in the region of Samaria. This was the land that Jesus passed through on His travels between Judea and Galilee.

Even in Jesus' day, the jealousy and bitterness between the Jews and the Samaritans that had started back at the time of the exile was still very evident. It was no accident that Jesus used a priest, a Levite and a Samaritan in His parable to illustrate the attributes of a good neighbour. In Jesus' story, the person who actually fulfilled the law of loving his neighbour was the Samaritan who had shown love and compassion to an injured man (Luke 10:25–37).

When it came to their religious pedigree, the Samaritan people were doubly disadvantaged. Firstly, they were descendants of the Assyrians who had brought their own idols and pagan practices into the land. As we have seen, these people then added the superstitious observance of some Jewish festivals in an attempt to placate Israel's God. This strange mixture then became their own religion. Secondly, Samaria was in the northern part of Israel, already separated from the southern Kingdom of Judah. Jerusalem, the city of King David and the city where Solomon had built the Temple, was in the south.

In Jesus' day, it was well known to both the Samaritans and the Jews that the promised Messiah would be a descendant of King David's line. Furthermore, He would sit on his throne, restoring the fortunes of Israel. Obviously, this had social and political implications for the Samaritans because if Israel were restored, they would be in a very precarious position.

As Jesus was passing through the region of Samaria, on His way from Judea to Galilee, He became thirsty. He stopped at Jacob's Well for a drink, asking a Samaritan woman to draw water for Him. This was unusual, as the custom was for Jews to have no dealings with the Samaritans – let alone a woman! Jesus then went on to speak concerning the lady's life, revealing that she had previously had five husbands and that she was now living with another man. The woman, perceiving that Jesus was indeed a prophet, then proceeded with a loaded statement:

> '"*Our fathers worshiped in this mountain, and you people say that in Jerusalem is the place where men ought to worship." Jesus said to her, "Woman, believe Me, an hour is coming when neither in this mountain, nor in Jerusalem, shall you worship the Father ... But an hour is coming, and now is, when the true worshipers shall worship the Father in spirit and truth; for such people the Father seeks to be His worshipers."*'
>
> (John 4:20–23)

As we have already seen, God wants to bless your particular mountain just as much as anyone else's because He wants to bless you. **It is not a matter of 'geographical credentials' but of 'heart credentials'.** Wherever Jesus is embraced by those who worship in Spirit and in truth, then His Kingdom will be established and His blessings will follow.

Jesus wants to set us free from our territorial and personal bigotries, petty ambitions and jealousies. When the Samaritans learnt that Jesus' face was set towards Jerusalem, their hospitality quickly dried up and He was no longer welcome to stay. The Samaritans were looking out for their own interests (Luke 9:53).

If your own 'heart credentials' are pure, then you will want to bless those who are worshipping God in Spirit and in truth, even when this is threatening your own position.

Jesus wants to set us free from aspiring to spiritual superiority over our neighbouring churches. His people should be one, even as He is one with His Father. Jesus has already prayed for us:

> ' *"I pray that they may be all one. Father! May they be in us, just as You are in Me and I am in You. May they be one, so that the world will believe that You sent Me."* ' (John 17:21 GNB)

There is freedom from jealousy, enmity, party spirit, factions and divisions. These should not arise between congregational flows, home groups, churches, apostles, towns, villages and denominations. Bless those who are embracing the Kingdom and worshipping in Spirit and in truth; bless those who are proclaiming the gospel, healing the sick or casting out demons; bless them wherever they prosper.

As Jesus truly changes our hearts, so His perspectives will become ours and we will begin to see more clearly His world-wide vision on our own doorstep. Each of us is His witness, *'both in Jerusalem, and in all Judea and Samaria, and even to the remotest part of the earth'* (Acts 1:8).

Chapter 8

Seeing the Issues

So far, we have looked at many factors in our lives as if they could be neatly compartmentalized or methodically stored away for quick reference. In reality, we all know from experience that life is anything but compartmentalized! We also know that everything we do, say, think or believe is added to become the sum of our lives. In the light of this, it may be more helpful to view life as a conglomeration of factors. When put together in any combination, any time, they will affect everything we do, say, think or believe.

For example, many of us will have happy childhood memories of taking part in various local or religious celebrations. These traditions brought with them a sense of continuity or belonging. As sons or daughters, we may have felt proud to follow in our parents' footsteps by keeping a custom or tradition alive in our own families. In this context, we can clearly see how local or religious customs can raise issues of family, inheritance, people, places and traditions.

Far from bringing us into legalism, reducing our mentality to a list of 'dos' and 'don'ts', God's heart is to give us freedom concerning these things. We are to be entirely unrestricted in every area of our decision making. However, if we do not see the underlying issues, then far from heralding in a new Kingdom, our religious worship may actually restrict us. It may reinforce a local or generational loyalty, in turn becoming a bastion of traditional values and beliefs:

> *'Don't become so well-adjusted to your culture that you fit into it without even thinking. Instead, fix your attention on God. You'll be changed from the inside out. Readily recognize what he wants from you, and quickly respond to it. Unlike the culture around you, always dragging you down to its level of immaturity, God brings the best out of you . . . '*
>
> (excerpt from *The Message*, Romans 12)

As the adopted sons of God, the good news of the gospel is that God has already saved us from the futile ways inherited from our forefathers (1 Peter 1:18). We are now free to embrace His Kingdom culture that springs from the life of God's Spirit within us, cutting across all the prevalent issues in our lives. God's way of life for us is founded upon the revelation that we are no longer compelled or constrained by the flesh (Romans 8:12–13). As we embrace the work of His Spirit in our hearts, we will become more like Jesus (1 Peter 1:2; Romans 8:29). No one is perfect, yet Paul urges us to keep pressing on to obtain our inheritance (Philippians 3:12). If we walk by the Spirit, we will not succumb to the desires of the flesh (Galatians 5:16).

As we earnestly seek to embrace the work of the Holy Spirit in our lives, we will find many of our natural characteristics and preferences changing as we conform to the nature of Jesus. **We may find, however, that some aspects of our personality are proudly defiant or secretly stubborn**. We may be opinionated and bigoted. Rather than reflecting the life of Christ within us, our prejudices and behaviour may reflect our very personal hurts, resentments or defence mechanisms. The Bible says:

> *'For though we walk in the flesh, we do not war according to the flesh, for the weapons of our warfare are not*

> *of the flesh, but divinely powerful for the destruction of fortresses. We are destroying speculations and every lofty thing raised up against the knowledge of God, and we are taking every thought captive to the obedience of Christ.'*   (2 Corinthians 10:3–5)

For each of us, part of the work of the Holy Spirit will be the tearing down of personal fortresses or strongholds that are not part of our new nature. This may be seen as a work of sanctification (Hebrews 12:14). When we start tearing these strongholds down with spiritual warfare, it may feel as though our very person is being confronted and attacked. This is because strongholds are often very deeply entrenched in our hearts and minds. Sharing these aspects of our personality with others is often humiliating and painful but this is a very real aspect of discipleship. We are not to be conformed to how the world thinks. Rather, we are to be transformed by the renewing of our minds, that we might actually prove the will of God in our lives (Romans 12:2). *'The way of the Lord is a stronghold to the upright'* (Proverbs 10:29). God is our true fortress, our place of security (2 Samuel 22:33).

Knee-jerk reactions are very easy to see in other people. They are not so easy to recognize in ourselves. For example, we may see somebody quickly flush with anger at the mere mention of private schooling. This will not be an instant reaction of the moment but the summation of their previous experiences that relate to the world of education. Similarly, we may suspect that we have an ungodly stronghold when we over-react. We may become unreasonably defensive or argumentative. We may even find ourselves rehearsing long speeches in the privacy of our own company! Most of us vehemently defend our own position when someone attacks our preconceived ideas or value systems. When we do find ourselves, or others, exposed in this way, the ensuing visible or verbal reactions may be likened to the tip of an iceberg. There really is much more at stake than meets the eye!

The outer defences of an ungodly stronghold seem to be pride and pretence. We simply pretend that there is no problem! We distance ourselves from other people so that it is not apparent. For instance, we may have a fear of outdoors. What will we do? If we can manage to so structure our lives that we do not have to go into the outside world then we will not solve our problem; we merely shut it away. However, if we really do want to possess the freedom that Jesus has obtained for us, we must abandon this strategy. We must recognize pride and pretence for what they really are.

Just when we may think that the outer defences have been undermined, what comes next?

Lofty thoughts! These lofty thoughts may be explained by reasonings or rationalizations by which we actually set ourselves against the purposes of God in our lives. We make quite convincing excuses for ourselves, using phrases such as 'Wouldn't you do the same in that situation?', or 'I suppose I'm just like my dad. I can't help it.' These defences of lofty thoughts may not be so difficult to tear down initially but we may find that they quickly erect themselves again and we begin to justify ourselves. We rethink the issue, spend all night working it out and come to the conclusion that we were right all along. There really is no problem! Just a misunderstanding. 'I'm not really jealous – I'm just not pleased that they can afford a brand new car,' or 'Nobody talks to me like that and I'm quite justified in harbouring bitterness!' The defences have gone back up; they have been reinforced, reasoned out and strategized. Proverbs 3:7 speaks a word in season:

> *'Do not be wise in your own eyes; fear the Lord and turn away from evil.'*

At the centre of a stronghold, there is obviously something very precious that we think is worth defending – something of our old nature that is resistant to change. We attack the centre of this fortress with prayer.

Although we may not always see our issues clearly, God can give us personal revelation. When this happens, people's eyes are suddenly opened, and they are able to see the issues and the truth about themselves. Often, they cannot wait to repent! It is at this point in spiritual warfare that the stronghold is rendered powerless, and if there are any demons present, they invariably leave. The fortress has been destroyed by the power of God; there is simply no place left to stay.

If we look at what we do simply on a human behavioural level, then we will fail to recognize the spiritual dynamics at work within us. If we do not put God first in our lives, something else will take His place. We may feel unfulfilled and restless, living lives that are without a sense of plan or purpose, looking for something to fill the emptiness inside. Whatever we may fill our lives with, whatever our perceived 'raison d'être', only God can fulfil our purpose for living, our purpose for being. God has loved us with an everlasting love, He has drawn us towards Himself with lovingkindness (Jeremiah 31:3). We are ever dependent upon His lavish grace and mercy shown to us through Jesus.

God desires to occupy the first place in our hearts; our first love is to be for Him only (Revelation 2:4). Who is your first love? Is it your husband, your wife, your children, your family? Is it God?

People, places, houses, things, philosophies and even forms of religion can all make excessive demands on us. We are constantly to be on guard against anything in our lives that could become an idol (1 John 5:21).

Whether or not we are aware of it, an idol will make unreasonable demands upon our time, our money and our loyalty. Similarly, an idol will constantly demand of us excessive devotion and worship. Idolatry also involves some fleshly desires such as greed, materialism, wealth and power. It may incite us to immorality, impurity, or even the worship of ourselves (Colossians 3:5). How do we worship an idol? By constantly making sacrifices to it. It is a matter of the heart.

Even our own value systems can become idols if we continually make sacrifices on their account. This may sometimes be at somebody else's expense. If your value system is clearly not bringing life to you, or to others in your care, then **God can release you from the burden of your own ideals**.

The Bible tells us that the way to become wise is to honour God. God is faithful and dependable and as we do our part in obeying His commandments, He will surely give us sound judgement (Psalm 111:7–10).

When God reveals an idol in our lives, whatever or whoever it is, we will need to repent, knowing that it is His very kindness that has led us to repentance (Romans 2:4). There may be sorrow and heartache, but sorrow according to the will of God produces a repentance without regret because it leads to our salvation (2 Corinthians 7:9–10). Jesus said:

> *'If anyone wishes to come after Me, let him deny himself, and take up his cross, and follow Me. For whoever wishes to save his life shall lose it; but whoever loses his life for My sake shall find it.'*
>
> (Matthew 16:24–25)

We have a lifetime in which to lose our lives. Each time we repent ... we lose a little bit more!

God gave our friend a picture of a beach. This is how he described it:

> 'When the high winds and the high tides came up, there were a few objects visible on the tide-line. It was possible to walk along and pick these up. As I walked, I realized that each object was something in my life; it was a problem, or a relationship, or an attitude that had been beached up. Then I realized that all these things were linked together. It looked as

if there was a long fishing line that was anchored somewhere well out to sea in deep water. I got hold of one or two objects that had been washed up. Normally, they were not visible because they were below the tide-line but God made them visible due to the circumstances. As I got hold of them and pulled, the line lifted up for a moment. I could see one, two, three, and more, hanging off the fishing line.'

This picture encourages us to deal with whatever God may expose in our lives. Don't explain it away. Don't rationalize it. **Don't weather the storm of thoughts that revelation brings, in the hope that they will subside again. Circumstances are allowed by God and under His control**. Don't wait for the tide to turn – some of these things are not washed up on the beach everyday. Seize them while you can, then the next one, then the next one … then the next one … Make war – not peace!

Chapter 9

Make War not Peace

'The Kingdom of Heaven suffers violence, and violent men take it by force.' (Matthew 11:12)

The Book of Joshua shows us how the children of Israel, in the power of God, took the land that was promised to them. They did not take the land by being passive; they took it by force, defeating all who had been living and worshipping there previously. They burnt their cities and pulled down their fortresses. Under the leadership of Joshua and in the power of God, they then overwhelmed the kings and amassed armies of the indigenous peoples, and won an entire military victory. However, on a local level, God's people were not so ruthless in carrying out His instructions. They put many inhabitants into forced labour rather than ridding the land entirely as God had intended.

As we look again at the story of the Israelites going in to 'possess the land', it is helpful to remember that *'these things happened to them as an example, and they were written for our instruction'* (1 Corinthians 10:11). We no longer simply understand their battles solely in terms of possessing a physical land; it is a type, a shadow, a picture of how we, as the children of God, possess our inheritance in His Kingdom.

Most of us will be familiar with the story of how God

delivered the children of Israel out of the land of Egypt. He did this by miraculously parting the waters of the Red Sea (Exodus 14:21–31). Under the leadership of Moses, God mercifully delivered them from the hands of their oppressors and enabled them to walk free. However, not long afterwards, they entered the wilderness and walked in a measure of unbelief. They grumbled and complained so much, that for forty years, God allowed them to wander aimlessly in the wilderness until a new generation was raised up. It was this new generation that eventually went in and possessed the land that had been promised to their fathers, under the leadership of Joshua.

God promised Joshua that wherever he walked within the land, it had already been given to him. Joshua was to be strong and courageous, being careful to live according to God's law, in order that he would be successful wherever he went (Joshua chapter 1). Following this revelation, Joshua proceeded to make plans, secretly sending two spies ahead of the people, so that they might view the promised land, especially Jericho.

When the spies arrived at their destination, the Bible tells us that they found lodgings in the house of a prostitute whose name was Rahab. When the king of Jericho heard about this, he sent word to Rahab telling her the identity of the spies and the reason for their visit. Far from siding with the Jericho police, Rahab actually lied to them, saying that the spies had already left her house when, in reality, they were hiding on her roof.

Rahab had heard of how God had previously dried up the Red Sea for the Israelites when they had escaped from Egypt. She had also heard of how they had been victorious concerning the two kings of the Amorites (Joshua 2:10).

Believing in the power of Israel's God, Rahab made a calculated decision based on her faith. By faith, she knew that the proud fortress of Jericho would soon fall into the hands of the Jews, even before God miraculously allowed the Israelites to cross over the Jordan onto dry land. In return for the kindness she had shown to the spies, Rahab appealed for mercy, asking the Israelites to spare her family when they eventually came to take the city (Joshua chapter 2). When this time came, her petition was honoured. Rahab was saved, along with her household, as she symbolically hung a red rope from the window of her house that was built into the city wall (Joshua 2:18).

In response to her faith, God was faithful to Rahab in just the same way as He is faithful to us. The poured out blood of Jesus is a sin offering for each one who, by faith, calls out to be saved (Romans 3:23–26).

The Book of Exodus tells of how, previously, the older generation had also sent men into the promised land, to spy it out. These spies reported back that there were giants in the land and fortified cities. Only Joshua and Caleb seemed to perceive that the land was actually potentially good to live in (Numbers chapters 13–14). According to their lack of faith, this generation was so intimidated that they missed their opportunity. Will it be the same for us?

The giants and fortified cities in our own lives are not insurmountable with the power of God. When we see the truth about ourselves, when we see the potential battles ahead, we need not be intimidated. We are to be strong and courageous, just like Joshua, because Jesus said that the knowledge of the truth would set us free (John 8:32).

In contrast to the older generation, the two spies who had stayed with Rahab in Jericho returned to Joshua, full of encouragement. They reported that the inhabitants of the promised land had already become demoralized on Israel's account. Full of faith and believing in God's promises concerning the land, Joshua then proceeded towards the banks of the Jordan, taking all the sons of Israel with him. God had already proved Himself to the previous generation when He had divided the waters of the Red Sea. Now, He was proving Himself to Joshua's generation. As representatives from each of the twelve tribes of Israel walked into the Jordan, carrying the Ark of the Covenant, God miraculously divided the waters for

His people again. This time, He enabled them to walk into the land to possess it (Joshua chapter 3).

Just like the children of Israel, as we go in to 'possess the land', to inherit our inheritance in Christ, our experience must be first-hand. It is for us; it is to be our testimony to our generation. In the same way, our children will need to see God at work 'first-hand' in their own lives and for their own generation. The basis of their faith will be their own testimony. The same God who divided the waters for Moses and for Joshua will be dividing the waters for them. He will be miraculously enabling them to walk free; to enter the land and to possess what is rightfully theirs.

Having crossed over the Jordan and into the promised land, the children of Israel then made camp at Gilgal. Here, they set up a memorial of twelve stones from the river bed as a reminder of the mighty power of God (Joshua chapter 4). As the news concerning the miraculous manner of their arrival spread around the locality, the hearts of the locals understandably 'melted' at the thought of the sons of Israel (Joshua 5:1). We overestimate the enemy. Even now, his position is precarious and he is in terror of God's people coming to possess their land.

As Joshua came by Jericho, the first fortified city, chapter 5 describes how he was met by a man standing in front of him with a sword in his hand. Joshua approached the man and asked him, *'Are you for us or for our adversaries?'* The reply was, *'No, rather I indeed come now as captain of the host of the Lord'* (Joshua 5:13–14). Wrong question, Joshua!

Similarly, when we face battles in our own lives, it is not a question of whether God is for us, whether He can be relied upon to back us up. It is a question of whether we are for God. Are we willing for Him to tear down the old so that He can bring in the new?

Whatever battles you may encounter in possessing your inheritance, the fundamental issue is that God's work in your life is always for your good. He is good to us. It may be convenient or inconvenient, it may be painful at times, but it is always good. As you take what is rightfully yours, you become more like Jesus.

Joshua then went on to ask the right question,

> '*"What has my lord to say to his servant?" And the captain of the Lord's host said to Joshua, "Remove your sandals from your feet, for the place where you are standing is holy." And Joshua did so.*'
>
> (Joshua 5:14–15)

When we are inhabiting the land for ourselves, when we see demonic influences being smashed and lives set free, we are on holy ground and God is sovereign. While it may still be true that we have ungodly strongholds or resistant areas of demonic activity in our lives, they need no longer control us. Jericho, the first fortified city, was tightly shut. Chapter 6 tells of how *'No one went out and no one came in'* because the local inhabitants were so scared of the sons of Israel. **As the army of God, our position is secure, the battle has already been won; it is we who are on the offensive!**

Having ascertained that Joshua was with the captain of the host of the Lord, God then went on to show him exactly how they were to defeat the fortress of Jericho. It was not by brute military force but by the divine intervention of God. As the Israelites walked around the city for the seventh time, when the priests blew the trumpets, Joshua said to the people, *'Shout! For the Lord has given you the city'* (Joshua 6:16). When the people shouted in obedience to Johsua's commands, the city walls of Jericho actually fell down flat so that they were able to go up into the city and take possession.

Will it always work like this? When we come across a stubborn stronghold in someone, it is very tempting to shout! We may even find ourselves stomping around in circles! It seemed to work well for Joshua, so maybe it will work for us! However, the Bible says that we do not tear down strongholds by human methods alone. It simply will not work because our warfare is spiritual. Again, it was not by brute military force that the children of Israel won their victory. Following their obedience, it was by the divine intervention of God.

Before Joshua went in to capture the city of Jericho, God gave the children of Israel clear instructions. They were not to sweep out the houses, keep the spoils of war or even to take prisoners. They were to do exactly as God had directed; no more and no less.

When we see our own ungodly strongholds being defeated, the same principle applies. We are to be obedient and radical, doing exactly as God directs. **We are not to be legalistic but led by the Spirit**. This will inevitably mean different responses for different people. For example:

'A number of years ago, God set me free from some issues to do with my past. Afterwards, I felt the Holy Spirit was prompting me to be radical. I had not heard any teaching or been involved with others going through a similar experience but I knew that I had to rid my life of anything that would hold me back. God was doing something new with me and I didn't want to get left behind. In this particular instance, I felt it was God's Word.

Many possessions had to go and I remember staying up most of the night, going through the attic, going through the wardrobe – I needed to be thorough. Among other things, there was quite an extensive record collection – quite valuable and of no intrinsic harm to anyone; yet I felt that they were to be burnt, along with everything else. I took them round to a friend's house as he had an incinerator in his back garden. As he watched it all go he found it hard. "Think of all the money" he said.

By the time I was finished there was not much furniture left in our house, not to mention books, rugs, or clothes. Money was tight, so I was not able to replace the stuff I had thrown away. Despite this, it really did not matter and was not important. In fact, losing material possessions was a small price to pay compared with the freedom God brought!

It didn't occur to me at the time, but since then, God has shown that he is certainly no man's debtor. He has provided abundantly, and I feel so grateful for the gift of his grace and mercy towards me.'

As Joshua continued to take the fortified cities of the promised land, chapter 10 tells us of how the Lord threw hailstones down from Heaven, killing vast numbers of the enemy. More people actually died from these hailstones *'than those whom the sons of Israel killed with the sword'* (Joshua 10:11). When God chooses to manifest Himself, His sovereign power is awesome.

Today, God is choosing to manifest his sovereign power in a fresh move of the Holy Spirit that is sweeping all over the world. As God's people, it is now our testimony that He is raining down hailstones! Just like the children of Israel, we have tangible evidence that God is slaying the enemy and fighting on our behalf. He is enabling us to inherit the promised land.

As God's power is released, there may be a variety of physical manifestations that accompany His work. For example, there may be violent or rhythmic contractions, bending double, bending backwards or bearing down. We may see writhing, shaking, flapping or bouncing. Uncontrollable laughter, coughing, groaning, roaring, hissing, or barking may be heard. There may be trances, an inability to move or deep sleep. What are we to make of it all? We may find ourselves asking questions:

- Is it God? (Consider that some leaders assume that they have 'bound' demonic activity before the meeting.)
- Is it the flesh? (Consider the extremes of emotional outbursts, the element of exhibitionism.)

– Is it demonic? (Consider the chaos, disorder, screaming and violent shakings!)

Rather than ask questions, earnestly ask for the
spiritual gifts as listed in 1 Corinthians chapter 12! These
include: wisdom, knowledge, faith, healing, the effecting
of miracles, prophecy, the distinguishing of spirits,
tongues and interpretations.

**The effects of God's power may be an offense to our
natural senses, but we are in a war-zone, and God is reviv-
ing His troops!**

For the children of Israel, there came a point in the
battle when God physically halted both the sun and
the moon, actually making time stand still in response to
Joshua's request. The children of Israel then proceeded
to make full use of this extra fighting time and eventually
won the battle (Joshua 10:12–14).

Surely, if we are serious about appropriating our own
victories, then when the power of God is sovereignly
manifesting, we will plead with God to give us all the time
we need. We will want to make the most of our God-given
opportunity to take more of the enemy's territory in the
ground of our lives.

God is miraculously changing us by the power of the
Holy Spirit. As He continues to manifest His sovereign
power to His people, so we are walking further into the
promised land. **We are taking possession of those things
that are rightfully ours in Christ Jesus** (Galatians 3:29).

Jesus has already defeated the enemy. As His sovereign
power falls like hailstones, so it enables us to walk in the
reality of His victory. This was our friend's literal experience. She had been walking with difficulty most of her life,
resigned to wearing special shoes. A battle of many years
standing was miraculously won in an instant:

'For almost as long as I can remember I had many
problems with my neck and back and had visited
Osteopaths as early as my teens for help in relieving
the pain. When I reached the age of about forty-seven

years, the specialist decided that the only way to help my back and feet problems would be to wear special shoes.

Not long after I had arrived at a church meeting, the singing finished and people all around me were praising. This was still a little strange to me as we had only recently started coming to church. I was just beginning to raise my hands in prayer, thanking God for being my heavenly Father and thanking Jesus for being my Saviour. Then my friend who had encouraged us to come to church with her, walked up behind me. She laid her hands on my back, then started praying and talking in tongues.

Without any warning, I felt my spine begin to wriggle. I felt prompted to move my right hip up. As I did this, I stood straight and without pain. I could hardly believe what was happening to me, as I had never asked the Lord to be healed. I thought the way I was was the way I would be for the rest of my life. I still could not believe I was healed, and I went to look in the mirror. Sure enough, my shoulders were level and not dropping some three inches on the right-hand side of my body.

The very next Monday, I had a prearranged appointment to see a spine specialist. You can imagine the excitement when I walked into the consulting room and put my special pair of shoes on the table. He was a little startled, but then proceeded to examine me. "Your spine is straight, my dear." He just looked at me in amazement.'

Let's be encouraged to press on! (Philippians 3:12). We may have a 'besetting sin', or an ungodly personality trait that we find difficult to control. We may have obsessions or addictions that seem to conquer us. We may be struggling with an illness. Do not assume a position of defeat! Rather, fight the good fight of faith (1 Timothy 6:12). **As we expose ourselves to the redemptive power of God, so we**

can experience His love and acceptance, His deliverance and freedom.

Consider this man's testimony:

'For fourteen years, I had experienced my Christian walk getting colder and colder. I had the odd spark of life, but for much of the time I felt spiritually dead. I was up to my neck in habitual sin, unable to break out and controlled by others. You could say that I was in a mess.

For years I had shared problems, sometimes from the heart, but I never seemed to get free. For example, I had wrestled with the habitual sin of lust – it controlled my life. I was also controlled by others, leaders in the church, seeking to please but being a "puppet on a string".

I had just returned from a management course on assertiveness. Obviously, my employer saw a problem. About the only thing I remember from the course was the feeling, "I can't do it, I need your help God." It was a feeble cry from the heart.

That evening I attended a church meeting. The subject was "spiritual warfare" and the aim was to win people for Christ. I knew I needed winning, let alone the world. One thing I remember was responding to the call, "If you want to be free, tell God." I did, in my own way, and nothing appeared to happen.

Later, we prayed for the leaders, during which time I began to feel like screaming. It welled up from deep within me. Without any counselling – I screamed, shook and cried "Deliverance and freedom!"

I have been free from habitual sexual sin for three years. At my annual review at work, my boss thought that he had invested well in the assertiveness course. I explained the source of change.

After this deliverance, this scripture came home with power. Ephesians 2:4–5, *"But God's mercy is so abundant, and his love for us is so great, that while we were spiritually dead in our disobedience he brought us to life with Christ. It is by God's grace that you have been saved"* (GNB). Our freedom is a gift of God, we can't earn it.'

Being engaged in war can be both emotionally and physically draining, but God has promised to renew our strength (Isaiah 40:28–31). Sometimes, it is as if God gives us 'time-out' during the battle to be overwhelmed by His presence alone. He refreshes us with a love that casts out all fear and doubt (1 John 4:17–18). As with the lady in the following testimony, God can change the innermost depths of our lives in a twinkling of an eye:

'One night, I asked Jesus to show me how much He loved me. I was really at rock bottom.

Suddenly, the world was full of bright blue light. In the middle of this blue light was a bright red light. This was beyond anything I had ever seen, coming closer and closer. All I could see was my hand up to Jesus and I was in ecstasy. A love "that passes all understanding" filled me and pulled me up into Himself. Never in my life have I felt such ecstasy. Each time I said "Jesus" more love than before came and filled me. I was surrounded by His glory and filled with so much love.'

God prepares a table for us, even in the midst of our enemies (Psalm 23:5). When we're weary of fighting, times of refreshing come from the presence of the Lord.

'I stood with my eyes closed, ready to receive from God. As I did, instead of being aware of other people in the room, I suddenly felt that I was standing alone in what seemed like infinity. I could see nothing all around or above me and as far as my eyes searched there was measureless, boundless, never-ending space. Just me.

Then I became aware of a brightness that illumin-ated this space and surrounded me. It wasn't a dazzling harsh light, but it was warm and felt comforting. I realized I was standing in the presence of God. Many thoughts went through my mind as I realized how wretched and sinful I was, standing before a Holy God who knew my every thought and action.

Then I heard a lady's voice say "Show her your love Father." Before she had finished speaking, I felt an incredible surge of warmth flow through me as God's love washed over. Again, before that "wave" had finished, another flooded over me, filling me again with a warmth and power. I stood before God in that infinite place and was just about to thank Him, when again His love surged through me. It happened again and again and again. Each time I thought it was the last time, but it happened indepen-dently of anything I thought or expected. It was God showing me that He loved me because He loved me, not for anything I did or said. It was just because He wanted to and had chosen to. God's love wasn't a human love – it was everlasting.

This realization left me reeling, almost breathless and incredulous that He could love me so much. As the tears came down my cheeks, or the laughter bubbled out, all I wanted to say was "You're so wonderful Father..." but the words seemed so short and insufficient and all I could do was sigh. Yet still God was pouring out wave after wave of His love on me.'

Let's now return to the book of Joshua. After the decis-ive battle in southern Palestine, the sons of Israel then went on to make war against the armies and major cities in the north. Fearing the victorious Israelites, the kings and tribal leaders of northern Palestine then made plans. They grouped together in opposition, managing to amass a huge army ready for battle. Despite the magnitude of this army, God miraculously gave the Israelites complete victory. This time, they were even allowed to keep the spoils of war (Joshua chapter 11).

When the enemy had been completely routed, Joshua took possession of the whole land, just as God had spoken to Moses. He then gave it for *'an inheritance to Israel'* to be divided up between the tribes (Joshua 11:23). Subsequently, the land had rest from war.

Although the land was now technically theirs to possess, it remained for each tribe to realize this victory in a practical way, at a local level. As each tribe was allotted their particular portion of the promised land to possess, it then became their personal responsibility to clear these towns and villages of the old pagan practices. This was according to the commandments previously given by Moses (Deuteronomy 6:4–25). It was at this final stage that the sons of Israel began to compromise.

They ended up only partially purging the land of its previous inhabitants, even though these natives were now largely defenceless. For example, the sons of Ephraim found it hard to drive out the remaining Canaanites from their allotted portion of land, preferring to put them into forced labour. Similarly, the sons of Joseph, also fearing the Canaanites in their portion, even suggested to Joshua that he should allocate to them additional land that would be easier to subdue (Joshua 17:16). The Israelites were actually in fear of the Canaanites because they had chariots of iron and were purported to be strong (Joshua 17:18). Despite Joshua's warning to cling to God as they had done before, the children of Israel began to flag.

In time, God's people gradually lost impetus in driving out any more inhabitants from the land, eventually settling and even intermarrying. **By ceasing from war, they had, in effect, made peace**. While the sons of Israel were not actively on the offensive, slowly and insidiously, the natives regained a measure of influence. As Joshua had previously predicted, these pagans became as thorns in their sides (Judges 2:3).

Eventually, Joshua called for a detailed report to see how the land was being settled, declaring that as for himself and his household, they would serve the Lord (Joshua 24:15). It was now the personal responsibility of each individual to choose whom they would serve. Joshua warned the Israelites, as did Moses before him, that if they did go after other foreign gods, then God would actually turn on them. He would do them harm, even though He had previously blessed them (Joshua 24:20). On hearing this, the sons of Israel publicly restated their allegiance to God and Joshua duly dismissed them, each to his own inheritance (Joshua 24:28).

Just as God won the decisive victory for the children of Israel, so Jesus has won the decisive victory for us (1 Corinthians 15:57). He has won our freedom from the sin penalty of death, redeeming us through His blood (Ephesians 1:7). **It is now the personal responsibility of each of us to make war – not peace!**

Like Joshua, be strong and courageous. Go in and possess your portion of land, and as you do, may God give you a *'spirit of wisdom and of revelation in the know-ledge of Him'* (Ephesians 1:17).

Chapter 10

Opening Blind Eyes

Now that you have read this book, we invite you to take a fresh look at the dynamics operating in your life. Step back for a short while and take stock. Consider, for a moment, some very basic issues that affect you. Think about where you live, your source of income, family loyalty and pride, your natural and spiritual inheritance, your family traditions and value-systems, your family hurts from the past or aspirations for the future. We have raised these issues because they affect us in our walk with God. When taking the radical step of discipleship, they have power and relevance. You may not have seen their influence in your life before – **but God is opening blind eyes**.

Here are some examples from a handful of ordinary people. Having seen their own particular 'issues', they have been faithful to declare war:

Free to be me

'For as long as I can remember, inside, I secretly felt I should have been a boy, rather than a girl. This was not something I really thought about at a conscious level – it voiced itself in my not really being happy with myself. I thought other people didn't like me. I felt empty – I suppose there was a lack of identity.

The most obvious fruit was that I craved acceptance and approval, particularly from significant men

– that is, Christian leaders. If a good word came from any of them I was really happy inside. If not, or I suspected they were upset with me (a frequent feeling), I was distraught.

I have been a born-again Christian for twenty years but it has not been until recently that God has started to free me from these negative feelings. By talking with Christian friends and receiving prayer, God has begun to set me free from the strongholds in my mind. I had felt like the person in James 1:8 – double-minded and unstable in all my ways. On one level, I knew God's Word, that what He says is mine, but on another, deeper level, there was a negative and destructive thinking system in operation.

Through prayer ministry, forgiving and releasing those who had hurt me and owed me a debt – emotionally and physically – I came to a greater level of security. The most significant happening for me was when I responded to the offer of prayer at one of our meetings. I was going to be a worker at the forth-coming children's camp.

Two friends started to pray for me. Then something happened that seemed unrelated. One of my friends said that God had told her that I wouldn't die if I came into His presence. I began to cry and sob and felt in pain. My other friend said that he felt that there was something significant about a baby. I shared that when I was nine, I had learned that I was not an only child. I had a brother who had died aged six months. Also, I really felt my dad would have loved me if I were a boy. It was as if I were a real disappointment, not being the son he had lost. That day, we laid my brother to rest.

I have forgiven my father for not loving me as he should and have released him from the debt of not calling forth my sexuality. He was probably so afraid that I too would die, that he closed his heart to me. Nevertheless, I needed his love and it never came.

117

I am still asking God to bring more of His King-dom into my life, but since that day I have been significantly different. God is good to me and now I know it inside. It's great to be me!'

Lord of my future

'I don't know when it started, perhaps I have always played these games in my mind. How could I kill myself? Not publicly, to draw attention to myself; but in a way that only I would know the truth. How could I make it look like an accident? No one must ever know.

If things got tough, I could play the last and decis-ive trump card. This card no one could take from me. I would rehearse the possibilities – just in the mind – driving the car. It had to be kept a secret.

Then God broke in. While I held this card, God could never be the Lord of my future. I saw that because I was always wanting the last say, it was pure rebellion.

I repented and confessed to others. I spoiled my secret. Once people knew, my secret was out and the power was broken. What sought to be my perverse secret friend – someone to rely on should all else fail, became by enemy. I renounced its attraction and confessed my sins.

Praise God He delivers us!'

No longer bound to be fat

'In a meeting one day, a word was given about God breaking in on someone with an eating disorder. Suddenly, I felt as though someone had stuck a knife in me. What was happening? I remembered that in my teenage years, I had sometimes made myself sick after eating. That was no big deal, was it? I dismissed the pain.

Over the next few days, I started to see that my self-image wasn't quite what it should have been. I was obsessed with how people saw me, even thinking when I met someone for the first time, "I bet they think I'm gross." Why did I think like this?

As a child, I had always been compared to my gran. I loved her dearly but she was very fat; I even called her "Fat Gran". All my life, I had been told I was her shape, had her legs and that I would be like her. No one said it unkindly, but they said it. I was going to end up fat, like all the women in my mum's family. I took this on board "hook, line and sinker" – even as a slim, teenage girl. I actually saw myself this way.

While we were praying, God powerfully released me from the strongholds in my mind concerning my physical appearance and my family inheritance. The very next morning, when I looked at myself in the mirror, in my own eyes, I had physically shrunk.'

Freedom is the jackpot!

'As a young teenager, I spent time with my friends, hanging out at our local amusement arcade. Here, we all enjoyed playing video games and gambling our pocket money on the slot machines. Rapidly, the arcade became more attractive to me and, although my friends would not always go, I began to spend more time there. It reached a stage that, at any given opportunity, you'd find me in front of a slot machine. Gambling had become a complete obsession that consumed all my time and money. I would go to any end to obtain funds to play even if it meant stealing from my parents, family and friends.

At sixteen, I joined our local Squash Club where I quickly discovered I could also play on slot machines. The Squash Club became a second home to me, and friends joked that I might as well "move in".

Some years later, although for various reasons I'd left the Squash Club and stopped gambling, there was something inside me that yearned to get back in front of a slot machine. In the Squash Club, I felt secure and had a sense of belonging. Losing hundreds of pounds on a slot machine seemed to meet a desire in me that nothing else could fulfil.

I had been a Christian since I was a child, but until my late teens, God had never played a very important part in my life. However, I now realized that I needed to be set free from these unhealthy desires.

One night, some friends prayed for me and immediately I got a terrific pain in my stomach. As they continued praying, the pain subsided and I felt numb. I had a sense of four walls and a roof tightly shut up. I realized that the Squash Club had provided a false sense of security in my life and I had been a slave to the slot machines. It didn't matter how much time or money I spent on them. I just needed to be there.

That evening God set me free. I no longer need to avoid the Squash Club or slot machines; I just have no desire to use them.'

Fear exposed

'I usually liked praising God – particularly when it got noisy – but this was too much. There were air horns, whistles, tambourines – even somebody with a dustbin lid. I was conscious of the expression "You're making enough noise to wake the dead." I was a bit uncomfortable on the outside, but on the inside I was really uncomfortable!

What was going on? I had the distinct jitters. In the church where I was brought up, the reality of "waking the dead" by making a lot of noise seemed quite probable! Not to step on the grave stones whenever you entered the building would have been hard! I remember the stone flags sounding hollow with the crypt beneath. I also recollect an unusual intimacy with graves – playing hide and seek among the old moss-covered stones.

When being prayed for later, I think I could have

scratched through the carpet with my finger nails – so desperate was I to dig myself out of the earth. The fear of death was broken and cast out.'

Run the right race

'From an early age, I lived under the shadow of an older, athletic, clever, popular brother. He succeeded at everything he did, whether it was in the classroom or on the sportsfield. Everyone loved him.

Although my parents loved me for who I was, and I had my own friends, I knew I could never live up to my brother's achievements and I felt very inferior to him. The area that bothered me the most was in sport. When my dad was younger, he had been a keen sportsman and I knew that he was very proud of my brother for his sporting triumphs. I tried desperately to join various sports' clubs, but although I got to play in some of their teams, I was never very good. I began to train in my own time, running and weight-lifting to improve my form.

Over a period of time, I became very fit. Although in team games I was little better, on a straight run I could beat anyone, including my brother! At last, here was something I was the best in and I wanted everyone to know. I would often run eight to ten miles when I got home from work. As time went on I began to change my routes, sometimes running past the home of the rugby coach and opposite my parents' house. I hoped that my dad would catch a glimpse of me.

I also became very strong in weight-training and started to enjoy training with others. Both running and weight-training gradually became obsessions. How far I ran or how long I spent on the weights, would be determined by my moods. If anything happened to upset me or if I faced anything I couldn't cope with, I'd go for a run – a long run. By the time I'd finished, I'd feel good again. This went on for several years and became a part of my life; part of me. I never saw that there was anything wrong or abnormal in what I was doing.

God, however, had other ideas. As I was receiving some prayer, I realized that I was guilty of worshipping my body. Not only was it important to run, or to be seen running and weight training, it was also extremely important to me to look fit and strong. I would deliberately wear clothes and jewellery that made me look good.

My friends began to pray with me and I repented. As I did so, every muscle in my body tensed up and became very painful. As God set me free, my muscles relaxed. God also exposed the root issues that had driven me to idolize my body. These were insecurity and jealousy.

Although God dealt with the spiritual issue, I also had to change my lifestyle practically. I got rid of some of my jewellery and clothes and stopped training and running.

Now I'm free to run or not, to weight-lift when I choose, and I'm no longer paranoid about the way I look.'

Guilty no more

'Though I confess it still hurts to mention "that word", it is only recently that the impact of what my wife and I had done many years earlier came home to roost.

Three months before we were due to be married, my wife-to-be discovered she was pregnant. All sorts of alarm bells started ringing. What would her parents say? Would they cancel the wedding? Could they handle the shame it would bring on the family? What would be the long term consequences for us? Would we be disinherited? To avoid these painful issues, we decided to do "the decent thing" and abort the baby. Despite being Christians, we were far too frightened to ask for help and had no idea that abortion equalled murder.

Recently, my wife and I have deeply repented of our sin, sought God's forgiveness and forgiveness of each other.'

Mixed messages

'Although I was quite unaware of the messages I was sending, I was actually conveying an emotional and sexual need from my personality. It has been picked up actively at least three times recently. These "responders" hoped that I would be open to an unclean sexual relationship because of the way they had identified something in me. As a man, the messages I had been sending out were obviously mixed.

The first was with a young man of about eighteen or nineteen. We had been friends, just playing darts in the local pub. He, unfortunately, had different ideas of the "friendship" and made a pass at me. I quickly pushed him away in total shock. I must have shown some kind of need to him and he mistook this to the point of thinking I would become involved in a homosexual relationship.

The second was while I was visiting another town for a few days. I stayed in a house where one of the guys seemed particularly interested in me. He seemed a friendly sort of person. He was affectionate in his words to me, but at the time, I was not wise to the implications.

The third was when I stopped to speak to an elderly man who seemed to have difficulty in walking. He was in town and I felt compassion towards him. After exchanging some words about how he was managing, he propositioned me, asking if I would like some fun. I immediately told him that I was not interested and that I was a Christian. Unless he was prepared to change his way of living and repent, I warned him that he would eventually go to hell. He then backed off and didn't want to further the conversation.

It became evident to me that I was sending out mixed messages. I needed to repent and be set free. Something unclean in me was being picked up by something unclean in others.'

Exposed to the light

'Growing up from the age of thirteen onwards, I felt drawn in my attraction to both sexes. There was a need to receive affirmation and love from another male, besides that which I received from my girl-friend, fiancée, then wife.

For many years, I carried this burden on my own, too ashamed to expose it to anybody, and totally unaware of how to receive healing and wholeness. I read a Christian book in my early teens, which gave me the impression that I would be like this for life. I believed that the "grace of God", helping me in this situation, would be the only way through my problem. It was something that had to be lived with and carried.

As I went from my teens into my twenties, I married and our two children were born. I finally plucked up the courage to share my situation with an elder of the church and although I was prayed for, nothing seemed to change. After some time, I shared the situation with two other brothers. Again more praying was done, but still no breakthrough.

I had always believed that one day the situation would be solved but all the possible doors were being closed off one by one and desperation was setting in. I began to lose hope; the feeling of despair in the situation was immense. I finally reached the stage where I felt that if the situation did not change radically, then I no longer wanted to carry on the lie and continue with life.

Watching television one evening, a programme was

advertised called "Homosexuality in the Church". I watched this with great interest. A particular person grabbed my attention. He was a minister of a church who had been very against homosexuals until his own son had committed suicide due to the pressures of being a homosexual himself. This event turned the father round and he set up a counselling centre to help other people.

I had to visit this place, so obviously, my wife needed to know before I left; I had to expose my true self to her for the first time. This was probably one of the hardest things I have ever had to do. I felt the shame and the deceit that I had brought into our relationship but this lifeline was what I needed.

I took a friend and we paid a couple of visits to see the man from the television programme. It helped, knowing that somebody understood how I felt. It gave me hope – knowing that healing was possible. For the first time, I began to understand why I felt like I did and what I had to do to become free.

Time went on and although I was considerably released, there was still a hold over me. Then one evening, at a church mens' meeting on strongholds and sexuality, I felt that I had to share my situation. It was incredibly difficult, as until now the number of people who knew was very small. I was opening myself up to a crowd of men, some of whom I hardly knew at all. Bringing the situation into the light was the key. Once I had exposed the sin to the light, the darkness had to flee.

From that meeting until now, God has affirmed me, changed me, healed me and set me free.'

Emergence into the sunshine

'While we were praying, God showed me a picture of an underground network of passageways, opening out into cosy little rooms at intervals. This was my home. Although the rooms were cosy, there were drops of poison on the floor and a rancid smell pervaded the musty air. God then showed me that all these rooms connected into the corridor of a previous dream and I walked down it with Jesus. The last door opened to reveal a large, central chamber filled with a huge and terrifying spider with poison dripping from her flanks.

As the people prayed in truths from God's Word, a dagger appeared in my hand and I stabbed the spider with it. She limped off down a passageway and I cried out to God to have mercy and not to let her lurk, seeking vengeance in a dark hideaway. Then the spider vanished. I turned and saw down the main corridor. The front door was open and light was flooding in. I ran and emerged into the sunshine, blinking at the brightness and fresh colours of everything (like Mole in *The Wind in the Willows*).

As I gambolled around in the spring sunshine, the burrow and passageways seemed to shrink away. I praised God for setting me free and felt a real lemon. Fancy living such a cramped and fearful existence underground when I could have been revelling in the sunshine of God's delight in me! The door of the stronghold of failure in my thinking had been broken. I would no longer be cheated of my inheritance in God, or paralysed by the poison of believing I was a failure.'

Let's be encouraged to press on! (Philippians 3:12). We may have a 'besetting sine', or an ungodly personality trait that we find difficult to control. We may have obsessions or addictions that seem to conquer us. We may be struggling with an illness, or feel the victim of circumstance. Do not assume a position of defeat! Rather, fight the good fight of faith (1 Timothy 6:12). As we expose ourselves to the redemptive power of God, so we can experience His love and acceptance, His deliverance and freedom.

Having written this book, we pray:

> '... *the eyes of your heart may be enlightened, so that you may know what is the hope of His calling, what are the riches of the glory of His inheritance in the saints, and what is the surpassing greatness of His power toward us who believe.*' (Ephesians 1:18–20)